CULTURE SMART!

THAILAND

THE ESSENTIAL GUIDE TO
CUSTOMS & CULTURE

J. ROTHERAY

KUPERARD

"The real voyage of discovery consists not in seeking new landscapes, but in having new eyes."

Adapted from Marcel Proust, *Remembrance of Things Past.*

ISBN 978 1 78702 296 6

British Library Cataloguing in Publication Data
A CIP catalogue entry for this book is available
from the British Library

First published in Great Britain
by Kuperard, an imprint of Bravo Ltd
59 Hutton Grove, London N12 8DS
Tel: +44 (0) 20 8446 2440
www.culturesmart.co.uk
Inquiries: publicity@kuperard.co.uk

Design Bobby Birchall
Printed in Turkey

The Culture Smart! series is continuing to expand.
All Culture Smart! guides are available as e-books, and many
as audio books. For further information and latest titles visit
www.culturesmart.co.uk

J. ROTHERAY is a writer and researcher specializing in Thai and Southeast Asian culture and religion. He has lived and traveled throughout mainland Southeast Asia since 2003, and has undertaken research on a range of subjects including the Pol Pot era in Cambodia, the film art of Apichatpong Weerasethakul, and spirit worship and popular Buddhism in Thailand.

COVID-19

The coronavirus pandemic of 2020 affected millions of people around the world, causing unprecedented social and economic disruption. As the impact of this global crisis continues to unfold, in many countries social norms are being challenged, and enduring changes will be reflected in future editions of Culture Smart! titles.

CONTENTS

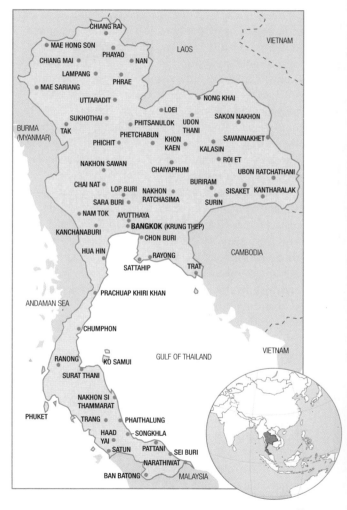

To many outsiders Thailand represents "the East" at its most beguiling and enigmatic. Golden stupas, green jungles, elephants, pristine beaches, a hot and spicy cuisine, and an even spicier nightlife. The famously exquisite manners and hospitality of the Thais adds much to this impression of an exotic Buddhist kingdom untouched by the passage of time. There is a lot to be said for all these things, but ultimately, behind the touristic facade, lies a country of 70 million people whose respect for tradition has in no way forestalled the advance of modernity in all of its guises.

Thai etiquette is rooted in a worldview that is influenced by the country's history, culture, and customs, as well as its longstanding interaction with foreigners. Most often its people are charming, gracious, and tolerant, and yet not every visitor feels at ease when interacting with them. Some are mystified by their seeming passivity and the difficulty of obtaining a direct answer. Others are surprised by what they perceive as an almost chauvinistic national pride, and a reluctance to acknowledge faults or errors. Moreover, there are times when the veneer of charm can prove to be paper-thin—as when you may have a brush with authority, for example.

Thais put a great deal of effort into social skills in order to maintain harmony in the public realm. To that end, they will generally avoid confrontation or criticism of others in almost any situation, even when it seems entirely justified. Their concern for appearances and formality lies in the fact that social behavior in public carries a weight that it lacks in the West, and what is understood to lie beneath the surface, in the private realm, is of much less concern. This can seem like a contradiction to an outsider.

Whether you are visiting for business or pleasure, it helps to be aware that different rules and standards apply. On even a short stay your experience will be greatly enriched by better understanding your hosts and getting to know them on their own terms. As their guest you will be made to feel at home—all the more reason not to inadvertently behave in a manner they may find offensive.

Extended sections on history, religion, and values will give you an insight into some of the complexities of the Thai psyche, while sections on daily life, socializing, and communicating will help you to participate in your new environment. Thai culture is rich and sensuous, and the many rituals of food, festival, music, and dance reveal a great love of fun and enjoyment of each other's company.

A final word about spelling. In Thai names *ph* is an aspirated *p* (not *f*), *th* is an aspirated *t*, and *kh* an aspirated *k*. In words transliterated for the purposes of this book the *h* is omitted. Thai official spelling is used for names, places, and festivals; otherwise phonetic spelling easily understood by English speakers is used. To help readers pronounce common Thai words, a system of tone markings is given on page 183.

Official Name	Kingdom of Thailand	Racha-anachuk Thai
Population	70 million	GDP per capita $7,792
Capital City	Bangkok. Population 8.2 million	Krung Thep (City of Celestial Beings)
Major Cities	Chiang Mai, Had Yai Korat, Khon Kaen, Nakhon Si Thammarat, Ubon	
Area	198,114 sq. miles (513,115 sq. km.)	
Climate	Tropical	
Ethnic Makeup	Thai: 78% Chinese: 14% Malay: 4% Others: 4%	
Language	Thai. Other languages spoken: Malay, Chinese, Khmer, Mon	Tribal languages: Akha, Hmong, Karen, etc. Principal foreign language: English
Religion	Buddhism: 94%; Islam: 4.5%; Others: 1.5%	
Calendar	The Thais use two calendars: Gregorian and Buddhist. The Thai Buddhist calendar is 543 years in advance of the Gregorian.	
Government	Constitutional monarchy. Parliament consists of a 150-member Senate and a 500-member House of Representatives, of which 125 members are elected by proportional representation and 375 first past the post. The country is divided into 77 provinces plus Bangkok.	

Currency	Baht	Coins: 1,5,10 baht Notes: B10 (brown), B20 (green), B50 (blue), B100 (red), B500 (purple), B1,000 (gray)
Media	The leading broadsheet Thai language newspaper is *Matichon*. The popular press includes *Thai Rath* and the *Daily News*.	
Media: English Language	The main English-language newspapers are the *Bangkok Post* and *The Nation*.	
Business Hours	9:00 a.m. to 5:00 p.m. Monday to Friday, except public holidays	
Banking Hours	9:30 a.m. to 3:30 p.m. Monday to Friday, except public holidays	
Electricity	220 volts, 50 Hz	Plugs not standard. Universal adapter needed.
Internet Domain	.th	
Telephone	The country code is +66.	To call abroad from Thailand dial 00.
Local Time	GMT + 7 hours	

CHAPTER ONE

LAND & PEOPLE

Thailand is a country in mainland Southeast Asia that is around the size of France, located in the tropical and subtropical zones. It is bordered by Myanmar (Burma), Laos, Cambodia, and Malaysia, and by the Gulf of Thailand and the Andaman Sea. The climate is hot, wet, and very humid, supporting a rich diversity of flora and fauna throughout the country's four regions, which were all until very recently covered with forest. Thailand has a population of over 69 million, of whom more than half live rurally. Although agriculture, mainly wet rice cultivation, was the primary occupation of most Thais up until the economic boom of the 1980s, it is the livelihood of only 30 percent today. Despite this ongoing trend away from agriculture as the country continues to develop and industrialize, rainfall and water management remain central and defining concerns for a country whose seasons are shaped by the Indian Monsoon.

THE REGIONS OF THAILAND

The Central Plain

Central Thailand is composed of the alluvial plains of the Chao Phraya River—the well-watered agricultural heartland of the old Siamese city states—and is where Bangkok, the nation's capital, is located. Established in 1782 on the Chao Phraya delta, Bangkok was characterized by its network of canal thoroughfares that also served to irrigate thousands of hectares of paddy fields. Today, Bangkok's sprawling metropolis is one of the world's most primate cities: all other urban centers in the country are dwarfed by it. Its official population of 8.2 million does not take into account the large number of rural migrants living and working there, to say nothing of the immigrants from Thailand's immediate neighbors who among much else provide the construction labor for the city's perpetual physical growth. Despite its chaotic form and sometimes shocking extremes of wealth and poverty, Bangkok is a fascinating city that rewards patience and exploration, and is surprisingly livable.

The North

The northern provinces cover the Thai highlands, a mountainous region whose valleys and river basins previously formed the kingdoms of Lanna, which until the early twentieth century were separate political and cultural entities. The largest northern city is Chiang Mai, with a population of just over 127,000. Although

Farmers harvest rice from the terraced paddy fields of Chiang Mai, northern Thailand.

it is being continuously diluted, the people of northern Thailand speak a dialect that is closer to Shan or Lao than it is to the official Bangkok dialect used in schools and on television. Their culture is markedly different from Bangkok's in terms of cuisine, art, architecture, and religious and folk traditions. The uplands are also inhabited by various "hill tribe" peoples who have their own distinctive languages and cultures.

The Northeast

The northeast, called Isan in Thai, is the country's largest, poorest, and most populated region and is home to a third of Thailand's total population. Those who live in Isan are primarily descended from peoples on the Lao side of the Mekong River who were forcibly resettled

by Siam in the eighteenth and nineteenth centuries.
Their dialect is very similar to the Lao language, as are
many aspects of their culture. Although agriculture
is the largest sector of the Isan economy, the soil is of
very poor quality and the region gets the least rain
in the country. Accordingly, the largest percentage
of economic migrants in Bangkok and elsewhere are
from Isan, and their distinctive cuisine and popular
folk music are known and enjoyed all over the country.

Peninsular or Southern Thailand

Southern Thailand begins with Phetchaburi
province, moving down through the Kra Isthmus and
terminating at the Malaysian border. The region has a
population of around 10 million. With the Andaman
coast on the west and the Gulf of Thailand on the

Maya Bay of the Phi Phi Islands, southern Thailand.

right, Thailand possesses some of the most beautiful beaches and islands in the world, although some of these have suffered from a highly rapacious and unsustainable tourist industry. National parks protect some of the most unspoiled and biodiverse habitats. The three southernmost provinces of Pattani, Yala, and Narathiwat are populated by ethnic Malay Muslims and have been under martial law since 2004 due to an ongoing separatist insurgency with complex historical causes.

CLIMATE AND SEASONS

Thailand has a tropical climate with three main seasons: the hot season (March to May), the rainy season (June to September), and the cool season (October to February). "Cool" and "rainy" are relative terms, of course. The average temperature in Bangkok in December is 77°F (25°C), but it usually feels much hotter because of high humidity, and there are plenty of fine days in the rainy season.

The climate varies according to location. In the mountains of the north the nights can be cold in December and January. In October severe flooding is likely to occur all over Thailand, especially in Bangkok. Areas close to the sea often suffer from high levels of humidity.

Peninsular Thailand has less sharply differentiated seasons. The southwestern coast and hills experience the full force of the southwestern monsoon between May and October, while on the eastern side most rain falls between October and December.

THE PEOPLE

Despite Thailand's cultural and ethnic diversity, the state's longstanding efforts at instilling a sense of national identity have been successful, and with the exception of the deep south, even those who retain aspects of another distinct identity also recognize themselves as Thai. Any demographic account of Thailand will usually refer to at least the following ethnic categories:

The Thais

Thailand was called Siam until 1939, when the country's name was changed to assert national-ethnic homogeneity as part of a project to modernize the country in line with Western influence. The term "Thai" therefore refers to citizens of modern Thailand, whereas "Tai" refers to the broader ethnic group to which the Thais belong. This group is distributed throughout much of Southeast Asia, Southern China, and also parts of Northeast India. Tai people began to move down into mainland Southeast Asia from Guangxi in the first millennium CE, where, over the centuries, they mixed with the Mon and Khmer peoples, adopting Indic culture and eventually forming themselves into city states based on wet rice cultivation.

The Chinese

In pre-modern Siam, Chinese merchants formed a special economic class, and the nineteenth and twentieth centuries saw several waves of Chinese immigration. Compared with some neighboring countries, the Chinese are remarkably well-integrated into Thai society, even though many retain aspects of their Chinese identity and traditions. When China emerged as an economic power in the 1980s, Thai-Chinese heritage actually became rather fashionable. Today, ethnic Chinese account for some 10 to 14 percent of the population, and are influential in banking, retail, and industry.

The Malays
There are over 2 million ethnic Malays in Thailand, most of whom are in the deep south, though there are some small communities in Bangkok and elsewhere. They are predominantly Muslim and speak the Pattani Malay dialect in addition to Thai.

The Khmer
There are over 1 million ethnic Khmer in Thailand, mostly in the provinces of Surin, Buriram, and Sisaket, which all border Cambodia. Though usually bilingual, they are completely integrated into Thai society and are considered Thai citizens. There are also uncertain numbers of Khmer refugees and immigrants in Bangkok and elsewhere.

The Mon
The Mon have been almost completely assimilated by the Thais, but a few Mon-speaking communities remain in the central plain and some of the provinces.

The Indians

There are around two hundred thousand Indians in Thailand, mostly in Bangkok, Chiang Mai, Phuket, and Songkhla. Many work in textiles and tailoring. Thais refer to anyone from the Indian subcontinent as *kaek*, which literally means "guest."

The Hill Tribes

The term "hill tribe" is used to refer to a diversity of ethnic minorities living in the highlands and along the western border with Myanmar. They include the Akha, the Lahu, the Yao, the Karen, the Hmong, the Lisu, and the Palaung. Whilst many communities have now been settled, these groups were previously nomadic and practiced slash-and-burn agriculture in high, forested areas. Though once they represented a profound challenge for the Thai state in the form of opium production and communist insurgency, they now form an important part of the northern Thai tourist industry. Combined, they number around 1 million within Thailand's borders.

A BRIEF HISTORY

Early Kingdoms and Culture

Official versions of Thai history usually identify a list of successive kingdoms and cultures that preceded modern Thailand. These include Dvaravati, Sukhothai, Lanna, and Ayutthya. In fact, relatively little is known about the earlier of these kingdoms, and some of them are subject to much national mythologizing.

Prior to the arrival of Tai migrants from southern China in around the eighth century CE, the most advanced settlements in present-day Thailand were Mon-Khmer. These were based on rice production and had adopted elements of Indian culture and statecraft through maritime trade contacts. The Tai gradually absorbed the Mon-Khmer and moved further south into the Chao Phraya basin, where a version of the Thai language we know today became the dominant tongue. Its earliest written example dates from the 13th century, in the form of a stone inscription from the kingdom of Sukothai that is presented in some versions of Thai history as a sort of proto-constitution. One section in particular is usually quoted in any account of Thai history:

> *During the time of King Ramkamhaeng this realm of Sukothai has prospered. There are fish in the water, and rice in the fields.*

The text continues to list the benefits and liberties afforded to the inhabitants of Sukothai, the paternal benevolence of its ruler, and its many religious sites.

Whilst Sukothai is often referred to as the old capital of Thailand, in fact there was no conception of a bordered country with a capital city until the late nineteenth century. The region was instead peppered with constellations of monarchical city-states (*muang* in Thai), whose prominence, reach, and stability were often short-lived.

Their societies were based on personal power networks, rather than centralized institutions. Warfare was frequent but the aim was usually not to destroy rivals, rather to realign the hierarchical alliances between these states. Populations were diverse and also very small, and when a kingdom did fall, its population was forcibly relocated to the territories of the victor. This kind of political structure is sometimes called the Mandala System. Having an understanding of this system allows for deeper insight into Thai culture today—see more opposite.

As the powerful Khmer Empire in Angkor began to decline in the mid-thirteenth century, the Thai kingdom of Ayutthaya rose to assume dominance in the Chao Phraya basin. Ayutthaya developed into a truly great and cosmopolitan city-state, not just through its military prowess but through cultural achievements and trade. As China's favored trading partner in the region, it supplied its giant neighbor to the north with rare and exotic produce such as waxes, bird feathers, ivory, aromatic woods, and other tropical forest products. Ayutthaya also took advantage of expanding maritime trade by acting as a hub between China, India, and the Malay states. In later times, this hub was also used by the Portuguese and other European powers. In 1569 the Burmese besieged and overthrew the city, taking thousands of Siamese prisoners back to their center at Pegu. Among those taken captive was Naresuan, a Siamese prince held as a royal hostage to ensure that his father, King Sanphet I, maintained his fidelity to the new Burmese overlords.

THE MANDALA SYSTEM

Before coming into contact with Western powers, the successive kingdoms that ruled Thailand, and indeed much of Southeast Asia, governed according to what is sometimes referred to as the Mandala System. Elements of this system are still observable today, both in politics and society at large, and being able to identify them can help in understanding those elements of Thai politics and culture that may otherwise seem inconsistent or contradictory.

Mandala means "circle" in the original Sanskrit and the system describes an entity that has its most powerful point as its center, and whose strength and influence radiates out from that center like light from a candle, growing weaker at the periphery. Power was characterized by personal networks, patronage, and a lack of centralization, and monarchs ruled through rituals rather than through bureaucracy. These city-states were organized into loose and dynamic networks of alliance in which weaker, smaller states paid tribute to larger states in return for protection.

Today in Thai society there are a great many vestiges of this system lurking beneath the surface. The importance attached to public ceremony and formality is one such vestige, the flip side of which is that society is much less concerned with policing people's behavior in the private realm so long as one's duties in public are upheld. As we will see, the endurance of "patron-client" relations throughout society is another. Underneath the appearance of modern Thailand's centralized political structure is a complex of personal power networks organized into a loose and dynamic hierarchy. This is one reason why laws and regulations are enforced to dramatically differing degrees throughout the country.

Naresuan made his way back to Ayutthaya at the end of hostilities and himself became king in 1590. His rise to power marked a period of successful military action against the Burmese, and the rapid rejuvenation of the city as a regional power, and today Naresuan is venerated as one of Thailand's greatest historical kings. There are hundreds of statues and shrines dedicated to Naresuan all over Thailand, many of which were erected in the last thirty years. He is usually depicted emptying a small vessel of water with his right hand, which symbolizes his declaration of Siam's independence from the Burmese, and his spirit is worshiped as a powerful guardian deity. His shrines are easily identified by the abundance of ceramic fighting cocks surrounding them—these are thanks-offerings given in exchange for wishes granted (see Chapter 3 for more on the importance of thanks-offerings).

A mural inside Wat Suwan Dararam depicts King Naresuan's entry to the sacked Burmese city of Hanthawaddy in 1599.

Over the following two centuries Ayutthaya again became a powerhouse of international trade, and a rich cultural center with a diverse population. Foreigners from all over the world were employed by the court to impart new ideas and technology in what came to be known by Europeans as the "Venice of the East." Theravada Buddhism flourished, and the monarchy and its rituals were resacralized along the lines of the old Khmer tradition: the king was shielded from public and his position elevated to that of a divine being. His power was ensured by his divine status and continued support of the Buddhist monkhood (*sangha*), and his influence further consolidated through possession of sacred objects and association with powerful deities.

After a century and a half of peace and prosperity, a new Burmese dynasty undertook to completely destroy Ayutthaya and take over all regional trade. Unable to withstand the unusually sustained nature of the Burmese offensive, Ayutthaya finally succumbed in April 1767, a date familiar to all Thais even today. While nationalist versions of history do not exaggerate the extent of Ayutthaya's destruction, it could be said that they have fostered a disproportionate image of the Burmese as the perennial rival and enemy of the Thais, an image that is still powerful in the collective imagination today.

The Chakri Era and the Age of Empire
The Siamese rallied under a half-Chinese general called Taksin, who became king and established the city of Thonburi, across the river from the village that preceded modern Bangkok. In 1782 Taksin was ousted by one of his own generals, the man who would later be crowned Rama I of the current Chakri dynasty, and who would go on to found Bangkok as the center of his new kingdom. Rama I's reign was an accomplished one. Siam prevailed militarily over Burma, and incorporated many smaller kingdoms in present-day Laos, Cambodia, and Vietnam into its power network of tributary states. Rama I also rehabilitated the Buddhist monkhood,

sponsored literary, legal, and manual texts, and reformed the institution of monarchy with the support of noble families.

All of the Chakri monarchs are celebrated and revered for their benevolence and achievements in official Thai history, but perhaps none so much as Rama V (r. 1868–1910). The son of King Mongkut (famous outside Thailand

King Rama V, also known as King Chulalongkorn.

for his fictional depiction in *The King and I*), Rama V ascended the throne at a time when French and British imperial expansion in Southeast Asia was at its most voracious. While a more nuanced version of history is warranted (see Further Reading), Rama V is recognized for presiding over Siam's endurance as the only Southeast Asian country not officially colonized by European powers. This was achieved through diplomatic means, and through the sacrifice of over one third of its territory to what would become French Indochina to the east, and the British Malay states to the south. At the same time, using his consolidated authority as absolute monarch, Rama V modernized

Siam's governmental bodies, infrastructure, and elite culture. Despite maintaining Thailand's political independence, the royal court fully embraced European norms, most notably in dress and in architecture, such as, for example, the Italianate Ananta Mahakhom Throne Hall in Bangkok.

Resentment of royal authority began to develop among a growing middle class during the reign of Rama VI, and, in 1932, the absolute monarchy was overthrown by a group of civilians and military men and replaced with a constitutional system. The military's almost bloodless intervention into politics in what has since come to be known as the Siamese Revolution set a precedent: Thailand has experienced twenty military coups since that year, more by some counts, and the military remains a major player in the country's politics.

The World Wars

Thailand remained neutral during the First World War until the last minute, when it sent a small contingent to France which saw action in the final month before the armistice was signed between Germany and the Allied Forces in 1918. This earned Thailand membership of the newly founded League of Nations. When the Second World War broke out, quasi-fascist leader Phibun Songkhram tried again to keep Thailand neutral; however, had little choice but to sign an armistice with the Japanese after they invaded in 1941. Phibun was sympathetic to the Japanese ideologically and tried to use the alliance to his advantage to regain territories seized by the French in the previous century. After Japan's surrender in 1945, the US agreed to look upon the country favorably in post-war negotiations in recognition of the anti-Japanese "Free Thai" movement, and its assistance of the Allied war effort.

The Cold War and the American Era

With the conflicts in Indochina escalating and communist insurgencies developing throughout much of Southeast Asia, the US invested heavily in Thailand as its primary Cold War ally in the region. This opened the country up to massive US military and economic aid, and committed Thailand's military dictatorship to traditional conservative values in the form of a rejuvenated and resacralized monarchy, and a virulent anti-communism. At the same time, American popular culture flowed into the country alongside its military personnel, giving rise to notorious R&R zones consisting of bars and prostitution venues that endure today among the tourist attractions of Bangkok, Pattaya, and elsewhere.

In the 1970s the US began to gradually withdraw from the region, and communist insurgents in Thailand stepped up their efforts in the north of the country. This tumultuous period saw major student demonstrations in 1973 and 1976, which both resulted in atrocious state violence and loss of life. The 1976 massacre especially is still a very uncomfortable subject for Thais and is rarely mentioned in public.

In the 1980s, prime minister General Prem Tinsulanonda neutralized the domestic communist threat by offering an amnesty, opening the way for a period of economic growth and prosperity. Despite ongoing political instability, the boom continued until the Asian Financial Crisis of 1997, which hit Thailand very hard. The baht lost half of its value and the Thai stock market dropped by 75 percent. The consequent IMF bail-out was seen as deeply humiliating for Thailand, reinvigorating a nationalist sentiment that outlived the country's economic recovery.

Mass Politics, the Monarchy, and Military Coups

Thailand's current political circumstances can be traced to the rise of Thaksin Shinawatra, an ex-policeman and billionaire business tycoon who was prime minister from 2001 until his ousting by the military in 2006. The only elected prime minister to ever serve a full term uninterrupted, Thaksin gained a huge following in the north and northeast regions through populist policies and rapid repayment of the IMF debt. However, his premiership was plagued with controversy over human rights abuses and charges of corruption, and he was widely perceived as a threat to Thailand's traditional elites.

Thaksin's divisive government gave rise to two color-coded, mass political protest movements that have come to define the period. The "red-shirts" were pro-Thaksin and made up largely of rural voters from the north, while the "yellow-shirts" were ultra-royalist and opposed to the prime minister, and drew most of their support from the middle-class residents of Bangkok and the south. This volatile period saw the forcible suppression of the red-shirts in 2010 by the military, during which eighty-five people were killed and parts of Bangkok's financial district burnt down. The monarchy's reputation also suffered due to its perceived opposition to the red-shirt movement which conflicted with its traditional position of political neutrality.

Yet, despite living in exile, Thaksin continued to exercise influence over Thailand's politics. His sister, Yingluck, succeeded him as prime minister in 2011 until her own ouster in 2014 at the hands of army chief Prayut Chan-o-cha, whose subsequent suppression of the Shinawatra power network was so thorough that

A red-shirt protester holds a portrait of former prime minster Thaksin Shinawatra and his sister, then prime minister Yingluck Shinawatra, 2013.

a resurgence now seems unlikely, despite Thaksin's resources and enduring support base. Prayut went on to become leader of the Phalang Pracharat Party and prime minster following the coronation of King Rama X in 2019.

The death of King Rama IX after a record seventy-year reign and Rama X's subsequent coronation were defining moments of this period. While arguments that the royal succession was at the very center of the recent political struggle have not borne out, Rama X's reign certainly began in a very cold winter for Thai democracy.

GOVERNMENT AND POLITICS

Thailand is a constitutional monarchy with a parliament consisting of a 150-member Senate and a 500-member House of Representatives. There is universal suffrage, and everyone over the age of seventeen is entitled to vote. Elections are held every four years.

Candidates for the House of Representatives have to be at least twenty-five years old and hold a bachelor's degree: 375 members are elected on a constituency basis, and the remaining 125 on a proportional basis from party lists. The prime minister has to be elected by a majority in the House of Representatives. To become a minister, one must be aged thirty-five or over. Candidates for the Senate must be at least forty and hold a bachelor's degree.

The Thai Party System

In Thailand a political party is most commonly a loose alliance of individuals and groups clustered around a key figure, not a coherent group with a particular ideological vision. Party loyalties tend to be fickle, with members ready to change allegiances at the drop of a hat, and most elected governments have been coalitions. This political landscape makes a bit more sense if we remember the Mandala System (see page 23): unstable personal power networks based on "patron-client" relations are a key part of the system and this basic structure endures in Thai society, beneath the façade of modern state institutions.

THE THAI MILITARY

After the revolution of 1932, the military took a central role in politics and established an unusually broad scope of influence throughout Thai society. The number of coups and military prime ministers since 1932 is testament to this.

The military and the monarchy have generally supported each other since the premiership of Field Marshal Sarit Thanarat (1959–1963). After a period in which military leaders had looked to fascist Europe for models of government, Sarit instead focused on the monarchy as an indigenous institution around which the Thai people could be encouraged to rally. He was instrumental in the rehabilitation of the monarchy during the early reign of Rama IX, and this cooperative relationship has continued to the present day.

The prestigious Chulachomklao Royal Military Academy has a curriculum that includes Management and Public Administration in addition to the more usual subjects of Engineering and Science. Powerful political cliques are often formed by graduates of the same year, and the Academy has produced many army chiefs and prime ministers since its establishment. The implicit philosophy of the Thai military is that their institution is an essential organ within the Thai body politic, which not only protects the royal family but also safeguards the nation against corrupt civilian rule. Therefore, military coups operate similarly to a "restart" button. If a civilian leader abuses his power for personal benefit, the military may step in to purge and restart the government, after a stabilising period of military rule.

The army owns and operates many businesses in Thailand, including golf courses, boxing stadiums, petrol stations, racecourses, hotels, and also radio and TV stations. Soldiers of rank in Thai society tend to be powerful and influential people who are connected at the highest levels. Reflecting the Mandala structure once again, these men often operate their own networks along personalized rather than institutional lines, meaning that factions develop often and easily within the military.

THE POLICE

The Royal Thai Police are an equally curious institution within Thailand's security apparatus. During the "American Era" and with the help of US aid, they developed into a sort of alternative security force to the army, with whom they remain in competition. They use military ranks and discipline and possess more combat hardware than is usual for police forces. They also comprise elite departments and paramilitary divisions, such as the Border Patrol Police, who enjoy royal patronage.

The police enjoyed a period of resurgent influence and increased budget under Thaksin, who was a police lieutenant colonel himself. This came to an end with the coup of 2014 and the present military-led government.

CONFLICTS AND BORDER ZONES

The Deep South

A separatist insurgency in Thailand's three southernmost provinces has been underway since the early 2000s. While the majority of the people in this region are Muslim, the insurgency is generally understood to be ethnically and politically based rather than based on religion. The origins of this conflict go back to the years following the Second World War, but a fragile arrangement put in place between the military and local leaders saw stability largely maintained. However, in 2001 the Thaksin administration transferred responsibility for the region's security to the police and dismantled the local networks and institutions the military had successfully established. Tensions reignited as a result. The subsequent response from the regime was heavy-handed and lead to several internationally decried atrocities. The military's remit was reinstated in 2004, but so far, to little positive effect. Travel in the deep south is difficult, when possible at all, and should be undertaken with caution.

Preah Vihear

A century-old border dispute between Thailand and Cambodia erupted afresh in 2008, leading to exchanges of fire and dozens of deaths. The dispute is based on the Preah Vihear temple ruins which were recognized as belonging to Cambodia by the International Court of Justice in 1962. They were eventually listed as a UNESCO World Heritage site in 2008. Thailand perceives itself to have lost both territory and face on the international stage, and the issue has been mobilised by nationalists. Access to the ruins is once more possible from the Thai side of the border, but visitors should monitor the situation and behave with caution and sensitivity at the site.

Myanmar Border Area

Ongoing conflicts in Myanmar between the military and various ethnic minorities there have seen a steady flow of refugees cross the border into Thailand. There are currently over 90,000 refugees living in nine camps up and down the border. Naturally there is a strong Thai military and police presence here, and visitors should be informed and cautious if venturing into the area—illegal trafficking of both drugs and people is rife.

Though the notorious era of heroin production in the Golden Triangle is over and the poppy fields are now filled with cabbages, a new trade in methamphetamine pills produced in Myanmar for the Thai market has taken its place. This trade presents no real danger for the informed traveler but expect to encounter regular army checkpoints throughout the area.

TOWN AND COUNTRY

Bangkok is by far the largest urban settlement in Thailand and is the political and economic center of the country. Due to its size and chaotic design it demands a little effort to become acquainted with, but its beguiling variety has a special character unlike that of anywhere else in the world. The name "Bangkok" originally belongs to the village that preceded the city and in fact is only used by foreigners. Thais call the city Krung Thep, an abbreviation of its full, 43-syllable title and the world's longest place-name! In translation the full name reads: "City of Celestial Beings, Great City, Residence of the Emerald Buddha, Impregnable City of Indra, Grand Capital of the World Endowed with Nine Precious

An aerial view of Bangkok's skyline including Taksin Bridge over Chao Phraya River.

Gems, Happy City Abounding in Enormous Royal Palaces that Resemble the Heavenly Abode where the Reincarnated Gods Reside, City Given by Indra and Built by Vishnukarm." Try saying that on one leg.

The old center of Bangkok is Rattanakosin Island, an artificial island formed by a bend in the Chao Phraya River. Rattanakosin contains a palatial and monastic complex, and is surrounded by districts of Chinese shophouse rows, cheap hotels, and a cornucopia of dining options, with much eating and business done out on the street. Less than ten

kilometers away is Rachaprasong at the heart
of the financial district. Instead of palaces and
monasteries, it is skyscrapers and giant malls that
make up the skyline here. Bangkok could compete
with anywhere in the world for extravagant luxury,
but part of its practical appeal is that there is a
wide variety of lifestyle options to suit every taste
and budget.

Millions of migrants live in Bangkok, many of
them in crowded apartment blocks on the outskirts
and the slums of the city center. Little effort is

made to conceal this profound disparity in living conditions. The city is hot, humid, and grimy, and its once serene canal system is now heavily polluted and lined with shanty housing. It is sinking at the rate of 1–2 centimeters per year. The city's traffic problems are a challenge even for the most patient among us, particularly at rush hour, when things can come to a virtual standstill. Thankfully, it is also serviced by canal boats, an underground, an ever-expanding sky train, and motorbike taxi services. (See Chapter 7 for more on how to get around.)

Bangkok has grown wildly and without reference to a grand plan. This has resulted in many of its problems, such as bottlenecks and slums, but also has given rise to much of its charm. Strange and beautiful sights await the urban explorer, and some districts are so leafy and peaceful that you may just forget where you are. In addition to its palaces, monasteries, and its wealth of restaurants, the city is rich in terms of classical and popular culture and has a dizzying variety of entertainment. Most districts are full of markets, pubs, clubs, cafés, spas, museums, and art galleries—not to mention brothels of every description. More on that in Chapter 6.

While other provincial capitals cannot compete with Bangkok in scale or variety they often have their own charm and are well worth exploring. Chiang Mai, the largest city in the north, has its own distinct feel and culture with hundreds of beautiful monasteries and a vibrant culinary scene. Korat, the largest urban center of the northeast, is noted for its Khmer ruins and national parks. Phuket Town is distinctive for its vintage Sino-Portuguese architecture, and its carnivalesque Vegetarian Festival in which parades of ascetics pierce themselves with all manner of frightening implements.

Relatively good-quality roads now reach into every corner of Thailand and travel is inexpensive (see Chapter 7 for more). In terms of architecture and infrastructure, the provinces have started to become more uniform in appearance. As in other countries, suburban housing estates and gated communities continue to eat up the variety of older settlements. Thailand's municipalities are officially divided into cities (*nakon*), towns (*muang*), districts (*ampoe*), and sub-districts (*tambon*). The smallest unit is the village (*bân/mìo-bân*).

Rural life in Thailand, though dramatically different to life in the city, has benefited from vast improvements in infrastructure, mobility, and education. A big effort has been made in promoting local products and attractions for both domestic and international tourists which has helped diversify livelihoods and generate new opportunities. However, it is also true that most young people in the countryside will make for Bangkok or another city at some point, and, though many do eventually return, encountering villages populated only by older people is not uncommon.

Agriculture, once the pillar of Thailand's economy, now accounts for less than 10 percent of the country's GDP. After India, it is the world's largest exporter of rice.

ECONOMY: THE BASICS

Thailand is considered a newly industrialized country, meaning that it has experienced more economic growth than other developing countries, and as such, its society has undergone significant restructuring. Thailand has the eighth largest economy in Asia and the second largest in Southeast Asia, with a GDP that reached US $540 billion by the end of 2020. The impacts of the coronavirus pandemic of that year are likely to cause a contraction in many sectors, though the long-term consequences are uncertain. Exports account for two thirds of the country's GDP, followed

42

by the service and industrial sectors. Before the pandemic, tourism accounted for between 15 and 20 percent, while agriculture currently accounts for less than 10 percent.

Though there is great disparity in both wealth and living conditions in Thailand as we have seen, poverty levels have fallen dramatically since 1980s during which Thailand experienced an economic boom. That said, there has more recently been a reverse in trends; according to the World Bank, those living in poverty in Thailand rose by 2 percent to 9.85 percent between 2015 and 2018. It remains to be seen when and how Thailand will succeed in reversing the emerging trend.

Thai family and village networks are strong and form a safety net for those who struggle to find income elsewhere. There is a strong sense of obligation among family members and help, when needed, will often be found, especially for one's parents. Many Thais in rural areas have mixed livelihoods, often made up of agricultural endeavors, cottage industries such as craftwork or pottery, and migrant labor. By not having all one's eggs in a single basket, one is better placed to withstand any economic difficulties—a lesson hard-learned in rural societies at the mercy of unpredictable weather.

SOME KEY DATES

11th C Siamese (Thai) people settle in the valley of the Chao Phraya River in Khmer Empire.

c. 1240 Foundation of Sukothai as independent Thai kingdom.

1275–98 Reign of King Ramkhamhaeng.

1296 Establishment of the Lanna kingdom at Chiang Mai.

1350 Foundation of the Kingdom of Ayutthaya.

1432 Ayutthaya takes the Khmer city of Angkor.

1548 First of the Burmese raids.

1516 Ayuthaya signs a treaty with Portugal.

1558 Burmese conquer Lanna.

1598 King Naresuan of Ayutthaya expels Burmese from Lanna.

17th C Foreign trade under royal monopoly developed with Chinese, Japanese, and Europeans.

1604 Dutch build a trading station in Ayutthaya.

1612 British open trading station in Ayutthaya.

1615 Burmese reestablish control over Lanna.

1656 King Narai ascends the throne.

1662 First French Catholic missionary arrives.

1684 First French embassy arrives in Ayutthaya.

1688 Death of King Narai. Siam expels European military advisers and missionaries, adopts policy of isolation.

1767 Ayutthaya is sacked by the Burmese. Taksin leads resistance and relocates capital of Siam to Thonburi.

1782 King Taksin goes mad and is replaced by King Rama I who relocates capital to Bangkok.

1821 British East India Company sends envoy to open trade.

1824–51 King Rama III reopens Siam to European diplomats and missionaries.

1827 Lao king invades Siam, but is defeated.

1851–68 Reign of King Mongkut. European advisers help modernize government, legal system, and army.

1868–1910 Reign of King Chulalongkorn. Siam modernizes further and develops railway network using Chinese labor. Becomes a major exporter of rice.

1893 Siam cedes Laos to France.

1909 Siam cedes four Malay states to Britain.

1932 End of the absolute monarchy. Bloodless coup forces King Rama VII to grant a constitution with mixed civilian-military government.

1935 Abdication of Rama VII. His nephew Ananda succeeds.

1938 Field Marshal Phibun Songkhram is prime minister.

1939 The country's name is changed from Siam to Thailand.

1941 Japanese invade. Thailand is forced to become an ally.

1945 Japanese withdraw. Thailand compelled to return territory taken from Laos, Cambodia, and Malaya.

1946 King Ananda dies. His brother Bhumibol succeeds.

1947 Phibun regains power in military coup, reducing the monarch to a figurehead.

1950 Enthronement of King Bhumibol.

1955 Political parties and free speech introduced.

1957 General Sarit Thanarat gains power in a bloodless coup. Military dictatorship.

1963 Death of Sarit. General Thanom Kittikachorn becomes prime minister.

1967–74 Thailand supports USA in Vietnam War.

1973 After student demonstrations the military government is forced to resign.

1976 Student demonstrations are put down by army. Martial law is declared.

1977 The Government is ousted by military Revolutionary Council in a bloodless coup.

1980 General Prem Tinsulanonda forms coalition and country stabilizes and prospers.

1991 General Suchinda Kraprayoon takes over in bloodless coup. A civilian cabinet is formed.

1992 Violent demonstrations lead to a state of emergency. King intervenes and General Suchinda bows out.

1997 Thai economy crashes. New constitution drawn up.

2001 Millionaire businessman Thaksin Shinawatra wins election.

2006 Military coup. Thaksin faces corruption charges.

2007 People's Power Party (PPP) backed by Thaksin wins election.

2008 Thaksin flees Thailand. Constitutional Court bans PPP.

2011 Thaksin's sister, Yingluck, becomes prime minister.

2014 Yingluck calls snap election, which is annulled. Martial law declared.

2016 New constitution passed by referendum. King Rama IX dies.

2019 Coup leader General Prayut Chan-o-cha wins general election. Coronation of King Rama X.

2020 Covid-19 hits Thailand, devastating tourism industry. New wave of youth-led political protests begins.

CHAPTER TWO

VALUES & ATTITUDES

Despite its rapid and ongoing modernization, Thai society is still organized according to hierarchies that date back centuries. As we will see, the family unit is paramount, and all social interactions take place within a complex order that is important to become familiar with. In this chapter we will also explore the most important and commonly held attitudes and values for Thais; being aware of these will help you to adjust your expectations and better understand the events and unfamiliar situations that you may encounter.

HIERARCHY, FAMILY, AND SOCIETY

Up until the late 19th century, social hierarchy was codified by the *sakdina* system which allotted everyone, from peasant to king, a number which dictated how much land they would have been entitled to own. While it first appeared during the Ayutthaya period, the exact origin of the system is unclear. Thai society has transformed dramatically since then, but its structure is still informed by a steep, if more flexible, hierarchy.

Whereas in the past hierarchy was based upon institutions of bonded labor and aristocracy, today it rests upon the template of the "ideal family." In the traditional Thai extended family unit, men take precedence over women (at least on the surface), and elders over youngers. The family cooperates in harmony and for the good of the group as dictated by its most senior member. Thai society is often explicitly presented in these terms; as a national family with king and queen as parents. Everyone has their own role and duty to carry out under parental authority. Within the national family, there are smaller families with their own parental authorities based on this same structure (here is the

Family members bless their elders by pouring flower-infused water over their hands as part of the Songkran New Year festivities.

Mandala template, again). This concept is supported by the Thai language itself, in which the speaker must select the appropriate pronoun to use depending on whom they are speaking to. There are over sixty such pronouns, and mastering their use is obviously challenging for non-Thais. Many of them are based upon filial relationships, such as particular terms for Mother, Father, Elder sibling, Auntie, among others. All of them, however, reflect the speaker's social status in relation to their interlocutor.

Class and locale are also determined factors in how people are perceived and interacted with. For example, provincial villagers who work outside in the heat of the sun are considered inferior to those in the city, where one is more likely to spend time indoors in an air-conditioned environment. This is the reason that pale skin is so highly valued in Thai society; most soaps on the market claim to feature whitening agents, and sunbathing is considered insanity. Broadly speaking, the closer to an urban center, particularly Bangkok, the more "civilized" a community is assumed to be.

As in any society, each social class has its own norms and etiquette, and the sorts of differences between them are not dissimilar to those in other countries. Unsurprisingly perhaps, there can be considerable resentment and ill-feeling among people of different classes and regions, and it plays a critical role in Thailand's politics. The powerful and the political elite are referred to as *pôo yài*, literally "big people," while the rural population is referred to as *chao bân*, meaning "villagers." Different political narratives mobilize and exploit these stereotypes to suit their narratives. For example, depending on one's perspective, *pôo yài* could either be wise and moral guardians, like parents, or they could be corrupt authoritarians. Likewise, *chao bân* could be understood as virtuous and traditional, or they could be childlike peasants just waiting to be manipulated by cynical politicians. These are generalizations of course, but as you become more acquainted with Thai culture, you may begin to recognize some of these attitudes.

STATUS, FACE, AND OBLIGATION

Due to the conventions of the Thai language and social etiquette more generally, acknowledging the status of people you interact with is more or less unavoidable, and indeed should not be overlooked. Not to afford someone the respect they are due, especially in public, would be perceived as an insult to their dignity and in most cases would require rectification of some kind. A deliberate insult delivered in public may well provoke a response way beyond what one would expect in a Western country. Manners matter!

In addition to the respect they are shown by others, a person's status is reflected in their ostentatious consumerism and material wealth. This is often referred to as maintaining face or *mee nâ mee dta* (literally "having face, having eyes") and in Thailand is done by driving an expensive car, dressing well, and having a large, extravagant house. Indeed, it is not uncommon for people of lesser means to drive a flashy car while living in extremely modest accommodation. In Thailand, maintaining face also requires making large donations to monasteries and ensuring through donations that funerals and house-blessing ceremonies are well attended by monks, and if possible, by monks of a high rank. Donor names are inscribed on buildings and billboards inside monasteries for all to read.

Another aspect of face is the studious avoidance of conflict, especially in public. Thais are extremely self-conscious about being perceived to be at fault or at blame, and likewise will refrain from making others feel at fault where it can be avoided. Being non-confrontational, Thais will often ignore the misbehavior of others even if it affects them directly and are less likely to make complaints about things like, say, poor service in a restaurant. Their response would more likely entail simply not returning to the restaurant. Public displays of emotion, especially anger or frustration, are unacceptable, and will make anyone else in the vicinity feel extremely uncomfortable.

Various forms of obligation are embedded in Thai society and the social hierarchy described. A deep sense of gratitude and obligation is felt toward grandparents, parents, and other kin who have given their time and resources to help raise and nurture children. This sense of gratitude and obligation, called *gadtanyu* in Thai, compels children not only to revere their parents and guardians, but to unconditionally support and take care of them in old age too—the idea of sending elderly parents to a care home, for example, is unthinkable. Openly disagreeing with parents or guardians is only slightly less unacceptable.

One is also obligated to one's patrons outside the family. In theory, people in positions of power extend help and protection to those below them, expecting loyalty and reliability in return. This patron-client relationship is responsible for the inscrutable mini-power networks that develop within and across Thai institutions and explains why official rules and procedures can often appear internally inconsistent. (See the Mandala System on page 23 for more.)

PRIDE AND NATIONALISM

Thailand has a strong sense of national pride that pervades most aspects of public life. It is systematically instilled from an early age and is a ubiquitous theme in popular culture. For Thais, great pride is derived from the country's Buddhist traditions and institutions, including the monkhood, as well as from the monarchy. Indeed, all representations and symbols of the Thai nation, from flag to stamp, are considered sacred.

Since the era of European imperialism that began in the mid-nineteenth century, the concept of "civility" has been very important in Thailand. Thais are taught that their kings, especially King Rama V, worked tirelessly and skillfully to modernize the country in order that a perceived lack of civility in Western eyes could not be used as a pretext for colonial conquest. While alternative views about the country's culture and history lurk beneath the surface, mainstream interpretations are not challenged in public.

While Thais are aware that, relatively speaking, their country is still developing, they can be sensitive to remarks that imply that their country is possibly less "civilized" than others. The nationalist interpretation holds that though Western countries may be richer and more developed in material terms, Thai culture is morally superior.

The national pride that most Thais genuinely feel is evident from how pleased and even moved they can become when visitors pay their country appreciative compliments and recognize its achievements.

PUBLIC AND PRIVATE REALMS

One fascinating quality of Thai society is the difference one encounters between public and private social activity. In Thailand, surface appearances and presentation matter very much, and public ceremonies of all kinds are considered very important. They are a lot more than just empty ritual—they are the very core of meaningful social interaction. This is a collective version of face, which requires conformity and sometimes an almost stifling formality, at least from a Western perspective. However, in the private domain this conformity is not deemed necessary. Thais are very tolerant of, or rather, disinterested in, the thoughts and actions of others as long as they do not intrude into the public realm and disturb the impression of harmony, superficial though it may be.

An example of this is the seemingly inconsistent attitude toward prostitution. While it is deemed both immoral and illegal, it is tacitly recognized and tolerated by everyone including the authorities, though referred to through euphemisms like "special services" or "soapy massage." Great care is taken by all businesses who offer such services to conceal their real nature on a superficial level, and though, while it may be transparent to all, at least appears to conform to consensus. Another example is the public consumption of alcohol after hours, especially in tourist districts. This is sometimes tacitly permitted but with the proviso that drinks are served in coffee mugs and that beer bottles are placed on the floor and not the table. Everybody knows that it is not coffee in the mugs, but at the surface level face is maintained.

It helps to have some understanding and respect for the distinction between the public and private realms, and how important collective face is in Thailand. Observing polite dress, avoiding physical affection in public, or joining Thais in standing still when the national anthem is played will earn you the respect and appreciation of Thais, even those who may privately harbor dissatisfaction with these norms.

PHYSICAL ETIQUETTE AND THE *WAI*

As discussed, the way a person comports themselves physically is very important for demonstrating respect and good manners, much more so than in most Western societies. For example, in the company of higher status people Thais will refrain from displaying an overtly relaxed demeanor or anything that may be perceived as informality. They will not cross their legs or lean elbows on the table, and sometimes will not even lean back in their seat. They will speak in a low volume and consume any food and drink with profound moderation. The most important principle to bear in mind however is very straightforward: height reflects status. The body itself is understood hierarchically, with the head being the highest and most sacred part, and the soles of the feet being the lowest and most impure part. In any formal situation, people will arrange themselves so that the eldest or most senior person is slightly elevated. If somebody else needs to walk past a seated senior, they will lower themselves respectfully as they pass. Because the feet are the lowest and least pure part of a person, raising them above the head of anyone else is completely unacceptable. Putting one's feet up on a desk, on public transport, or in any situation where the soles are facing another person is extremely offensive and will rarely be tolerated. In the most unequal situations, such as between monk and layperson, or royalty and commoner, breaking this physical etiquette is actually illegal and carries serious consequences. It is important to remember that even representations of monks and royalty, in this context, are considered no different from the real thing. This includes images, statues, symbols of all kinds, even coins, as they show the king's face: never step on a coin!

The universal Thai greeting is the *wai* (pronounced *wâi*)—a prayer-like gesture made by closing the hands together flat and raising them up in front of you. Depending on context, this can be done silently, or accompanied by a greeting or thanks. The height to which you raise your hands will depend on the status of the person to whom you are offering the *wai*; for example, an adult returning a child's *wai* would keep their hands very low. The child, however, would raise their hands up in front of their face while bowing their head slightly as well. It takes time to learn how to *wai* in different situations, and the safest strategy is simply to return a *wai* in the same form as it is offered to you, unless the person is much younger than you. Thais certainly appreciate foreigners making the effort to *wai*, but they won't expect nuance or perfection. Don't overuse the gesture, however. Once upon meeting and again when leaving is ample. Otherwise, it is appropriate to offer a *wai* when somebody does you a favor or helps you out—you can offer a *wai* and say thank you, which is pronounced *kòp koon kúp* for male speakers, and *kòp koon kâ* for female speakers.

There are numerous ideas that contribute to the head being sacred, some of which are rooted in older, pre-Buddhist beliefs associated with *kwǎn*. *Kwǎn* are the soul-like constituents of each person and which

number thirty-two in total. In past times, illness and malady were attributed to *kwăn* leaving the body and becoming lost, requiring a special ritual to restore them. Not only is the head the seat of many of these *kwăn*, but all of them enter and leave the body via the crown of the head. While many Thais now find these ideas quaint, the taboo associated with touching the crown of the head still holds, and only people who are very intimate with each other will ignore it.

Custom dictates that you should not offer or receive things with your left hand. This originates from the tradition that in Thailand the left hand is used for ablutions after using the toilet. The left-handed need not worry, however. In most interactions, particularly with foreigners who are known to have different toilet habits, few Thais will be offended if you have to use your left hand when passing them something. As more of the country continues to adopt Western-style plumbing and bathroom design, this custom is likely to continue to fade.

FUN, SMILES, AND GENEROSITY

Thais place a lot of value on having fun (*sanùk*), which usually involves large groups of people and loud music. Day trips, holidays, house-blessing parties, temple fairs, and often funerals all typically involve karaoke with huge sound systems, lots of food and drink, and as many people as possible. This collective and voluminous release is an important part of Thai social behavior.

There is, however, a myth that Thais are so given over to constant *sanùk* that they will shirk any other activity. The word in Thai for work is the same word as for party, as many travel guides like to point out. Well, the word is the same, but it actually refers to any collective activity or event, and by no means does it guarantee or imply that fun will be had. Nonetheless, work schedules for the majority of the population are long and grueling, and this is perhaps why Thais like to spend some of their free time cutting loose.

At the risk of disappointing anyone, it must be said that Thailand's international calling card as the "Land of Smiles" is but a successful marketing strategy launched by the tourism industry in the hope of communicating the Thai genius for hospitality and evoking a sense of "oriental mystique." In truth, Thais are not more prone to smiling than anyone else, and its action has no unique function or coded meaning here, though a person may smile when they feel awkward. Care and attention to hospitality certainly is a Thai characteristic, however, and the country boasts some of the most acclaimed hotels and resorts in the world.

Thais are often remarkably generous in every sense of the word. They will often go out of their way to help when it is needed, they are excellent hosts, and as far as possible will spare no expense when hosting friends. The idea of disciplined saving is not a popular one, and if someone has just been paid or has otherwise come into money, they will tend to throw it around for as long as it lasts rather than tuck it away for a rainy day.

ATTITUDES TO SEX

Thais today have quite a progressive attitude to sex, although by and large men still get the better end of the deal. Institutionalized polygamy among the elite classes survived into the twentieth century, and it lives on still just below the surface. It is still considered a convention for any powerful man to have girlfriends and minor wives set up in apartments and small houses. Even rural locations are well stocked with love hotels, which charge by the hour and pull a curtain across visitors' cars in order to allow its passengers to enter and leave discreetly. Prostitution of all imaginable forms is ubiquitous, but only a slim percentage of the market is tourist-orientated. As mentioned above, despite this ubiquity, it remains a taboo subject in public.

Sex between couples in private is considered their business, and today Thai parents are a great deal more tolerant of older teenage children having casual boyfriends and girlfriends than the generation before were. Again, what is undertaken discreetly and behind closed doors, and which does not cause any public embarrassment, is generally seen as nobody else's concern.

Public attitudes toward sex, however, especially among the middle classes, can appear almost Victorian in their sense of propriety. Thai TV soap operas are a good example of this. Attitudes in rural areas can be just as conservative, but there is also a bawdier tradition to be found in rural pop culture. This can be observed in many places, from fairgrounds to temple murals.

ATTITUDES TO FOREIGNERS

By and large, Thai people are almost supernaturally tolerant of foreigners. They refer to Caucasian Westerners as *faràng*, and are insensitive to the cultural differences within this broad ethnic category. In popular culture *faràng* may be depicted as "imperialist wolves" menacing the "Siamese lamb," or else well-mannered bringers of investment, aid, and material prosperity. Despite the historical period that may be referenced, no hostility or resentment is ever promoted or encouraged. For thirty years or more *faràng* have been a constant, varied, and voluminous tourist presence in the country, and will excite no special attention in areas with tourist attractions. Off the beaten track there will be more interest: people will look, smile, and the braver ones will approach and try out any English they may know. In these sorts of encounters, don't be offended if you are asked unusually personal questions. You can answer these any way you wish.

Foreigners can offend Thais by dressing immodestly (in general, that means making sure your shoulders and knees are covered), not observing Thai manners, or disrespecting Thai culture or customs. You may find people who deal with rowdy tourists on a daily basis to be gruffer than others, despite your best efforts. Warranted or not, there is a perception of backpackers and young shoestring travelers as being unhygienic and stingy, and while it's certainly acceptable to sweat in the heat, not washing or grooming yourself regularly will quickly put people off. (It is not unusual for some first-time visitors to feel the need to shower several times a day due to the heat and humidity.) Being clean, modest, friendly, and respectful will all go a long way toward ensuring positive interactions in Thailand.

Marriages, casual relationships, and friendships between Thais and foreigners are all considered acceptable today, though there may yet be some stigma attached to a relationship between an older foreign man and a visibly younger Thai woman, but on the whole this won't inspire anything more than gossip about how and where the couple met.

Today, *faràng* are beginning to be overtaken in Thailand by Chinese visitors, who are arriving to the country in ever greater numbers. As China's presence and influence continues to grow throughout Southeast Asia, it will be interesting to observe how it may alter attitudes toward Westerners, if at all.

Black and Asian visitors should expect no discrimination in Thailand, although Thais may be less aware of the social issues surrounding ethnic identities in Western countries. Crude national stereotypes, for example, are regularly indulged in popular culture.

As with elsewhere, the coronavirus pandemic has made Thais slightly more wary of foreigners for the time being, and visitors should take care to respect and follow whatever health and safety rules are in place in the country at the time of visiting, even if these seem superficial and ineffective. The rules are often different in every province.

CHANGING TIMES

Societal pressure to conform is substantial in Thailand, and in general, its education system does not encourage critical thinking. Nonetheless, values and attitudes are changing rapidly, and as younger and more progressive Thais take up positions of influence there is hope that they will tackle some of the more regressive tendencies in Thai politics and society, such as cronyism and corruption.

Traditional family and community structures are gradually corroding as Thailand shifts to an economy that is that once more globally and individually orientated. This process is part of why Thailand is so attractive to visitors; Thais are open-minded, flexible, and pragmatic in addition to maintaining a deep respect for tradition. This is reflected in another oft-quoted Thai national trait: the ability to pick and choose the beneficial aspects of foreign cultures while retaining the best aspects of one's own.

CHAPTER THREE

RELIGION, CUSTOMS, & TRADITIONS

Religion in Thailand is much more flexible and fluid than it has become in the West. As such, it is able to move with and reflect the changing values and concerns of contemporary Thai society quite accurately. As we have seen, Buddhism is central to Thai culture and identity, and provides inspiration for much of the country's art and architecture, and gives form to its worldview. Thailand sees itself as the center of Theravada Buddhism, a conservative form of Buddhism which gives preeminence to the Pali language versions of the Buddhist scriptures. However, first-time visitors who know this are often surprised to see a lot of religious behavior in Thailand that doesn't appear to be very conservative, or even very Buddhist. This is because Thai Buddhism as it is practiced today is actually a syncretic mixture of several different traditions. These include Brahmanism, spirit worship, royalism, folklore, and magic, all blended together inside an overarching Buddhist framework.

Having a basic grasp of what's what in the colorful and omnipresent world of Thai religion will give you valuable insight into the Thai worldview.

BUDDHISM

Doctrinal Ideals and Social Reality

What is Buddhism? According to legend, the Buddha, or "enlightened one," was an Indian prince named Gautama Siddhartha (c. 563–483 BCE), who lived on the Indian–Nepalese border. After renouncing the privileges of his rank to become a hermit, he started to meditate on the suffering he saw around him and

sought to discover its root causes. Eventually he attained the state of enlightenment (*nirvana*) under a banyan tree, and in so doing escaped the cycle of rebirth and suffering that is the lot of all sentient beings. For the rest of his life he traveled on foot and spread his doctrine, which is called *dharma*, or in Thai, *tamá*.

A Buddha statue in Wat Umong, Chiang Mai.

Buddhist thought acknowledges that all living beings are reborn after death in different forms that reflect their karmic balance. *Karma* is the idea that all action has a consequence and moral value, which accumulate and result in either a better or worse rebirth somewhere on the hierarchy of sentient life. According to Theravada Buddhism as practiced in Thailand, high status men are at the top of the hierarchy, while the lowest and least graceful animals are at the bottom. The ultimate goal in Buddhism is to escape the cycle of rebirth and achieve enlightenment. In practice, most are simply trying to accrue as much good karma as possible to improve their chances of a good rebirth. This is done through committing to the Buddhist precepts (see below), and actively "making merit" by supporting the monkhood (*sangha*) through various forms of donations. Other rituals such as releasing captive animals are also believed to generate merit.

THE FIVE LAY BUDDHIST PRECEPTS

- To abstain from taking life.
- To abstain from taking what is not given.
- To abstain from sensuous misconduct.
- To abstain from false speech.
- To abstain from intoxicants that cloud the mind.

Wat Phra Singh in Chiang Mai, northern Thailand.

Though some of the precepts, such as avoiding alcohol, may be more honored in the breach than in the observance, it is not uncommon for people to commit to undertake one or another of them for a set period of time.

Insight meditation *(vipassana)* is an increasingly ubiquitous aspect of popular practice, and there are many monastic and lay organizations who teach this discipline to people from all walks of life. Many of them also offer English-language courses geared towards foreigners who wish to improve their practice or commit to lengthy retreats in forest monasteries. Some Thais view meditation as the preserve of monks and focus instead on making regular donations.

Apart from offering moral and spiritual guidance, institutional Buddhism also plays a broader social role, though its influence has waned in recent decades. In villages and towns throughout Thailand monasteries maintain a similar function to that of community centers, whereby they may host festivals, fairs, and communal ceremonies, as well as provide a focal point for the community's welfare efforts. At one time, monasteries were the only organizations offering schooling, secular as well as religious, though only to boys. In some areas this is still the case.

Another Buddhist influence is the use of the Buddhist calendar in parallel with the Gregorian calendar that is used in the West. The Buddhist calendar is 543 years in advance of the latter, so the year 2000 was 2543 BE (Buddhist Era)—the year zero represents that of the Buddha's death.

The Monastic Tradition

The *sangha* exists to preserve the Buddha's teachings and to act as a "field of merit" for laypeople. It is still a convention in Thailand for every male to ordain as a monk for at least one Vassa (Buddhist Lent) which consists of a three-month retreat over the rainy season. Many ordain for much shorter periods, however, and may do so repeatedly over the course of their lives. Monks dress in saffron robes and renounce personal possessions for as long as they are ordained. They rise at 4:00 a.m. to chant and set out an hour later to collect alms, a common sight throughout Thailand, until around 7:00 a.m. Monks are not allowed to eat after midday, though they may have sweetened drinks.

As the *sangha* depends on the lay community, offering alms is one of the most important and common ways for lay people to make merit. Everything a monk will use is donated, from their robes to the bricks of the cells that they live in.

Women are not permitted to ordain as monks but may ordain as *mâe chi*. You can identify these female monastics by their shaved heads and white robes. They are not subject to the exemptions and support that the state offers monks and are of a much lower status.

In Thailand there are different attitudes and traditions within the *sangha*. Some monks achieve a status that is comparable to sainthood and accrue large followings of devotees. Others run their monasteries almost as businesses, selling amulets, statuettes, and

Making merit: villagers offer food to monks on their daily alms round.

other magical objects. Still others avoid laypeople as much as possible to live contemplative lives in remote forest monasteries or wandering through the countryside.

Monks reside in monasteries (*wát*) which are found in every community. They have a very distinctive architectural style, featuring multitiered roofs with glazed tiles and elegant finials that sparkle in the tropical sunlight. Whilst monasteries can differ enormously in their content, all have the following basic features:

- Ordination Hall (*bòt/ubosòt*) – The most important part of a monastery. A relatively small structure used for ordaining ceremonies, surrounded by eight *sima* or boundary stones.
- Preaching Hall (*wihǎn*) – Usually the largest structure in the complex, this features a central Buddha image and is used for preaching, chanting, and other ceremonies. Thai visitors will usually head here first to prostrate and ask for blessings from the Buddha.
- Stupa (*chedi*) – A large conical structure that contains a relic, either from the Buddha himself, or more usually, a local saint.
- Bodhi Tree (*Dtôn po*) – The tree with the heart-shaped leaf under which the Buddha became enlightened. People donate sticks to support the tree in order to make merit.
- Pavilion (*sǎla*) – Open-walled structure for ceremonies.
- Library (*hǒ dtrai*) – These are usually tiny rooms on stilts in a pond or inside a moat to protect the palm-leaf manuscripts from insects. Not all monasteries have a library.

Many monasteries also contain shrines to a variety of spirits and deities in addition to the Buddha. (See more on spirit worship below.) More rarely, monasteries may contain a museum. Sometimes these are dedicated to a local saint, other times they are more like collections of curiosities and antiques. Because of the emphasis on donation in Thai Buddhism, monasteries often become the terminus for all manner of random *objet d'art*.

BRAHMANISM

In addition to Buddhism, the Thai tradition has absorbed many other elements of Indian high culture. For example, Brahmins have held a ceremonial role in Thai royal courts since before the Ayutthaya period, and their roles were even expanded during the recent reign of Rama IX (1946–2016).

In addition, localized versions of Indian literature have become an important element of the Thai royal tradition, particularly the Ramayana (Ramakien). The Chakri kings are referred to as "Rama," and the country's most important Buddha image, the Emerald Buddha, is housed in a room whose walls are covered in murals depicting scenes from the Sanskrit epic.

Many other genres of traditional knowledge in Thailand, such as medicine and therapeutic massage, also originate from India. Wat Pho in Bangkok, for example, contains a massage school, teaches traditional

Dancers at the Brahman Erawan Shrine in Pratunam, central Bangkok.

medicine, and has on display a number of educational murals in addition to its enormous reclining Buddha.

You will also often see deities from the Hindu pantheon in shrines all over the country. Most common are Indra, Brahma, Ganesh, Shiva, and Vishnu. Indian-style hermits or forest ascetics dressed in animal skins also play a role in Thai mythical and religious traditions, and their shrines are found in caves and on mountains, particularly in the north. Thais view these deities as part of the Buddhist universe, and most see no inconsistency in worshiping them or showing them respect.

THE SPIRIT PANTHEON

Spirit worship predates the arrival of Indian culture in Southeast Asia. Unlike the spread of Christianity in Europe, the establishment of Buddhism in Thailand did not result in the suppression of indigenous religious practices. Rather, these practices were absorbed within a Buddhist framework. Popular opinions vary on the status of spirit worship, but it is ubiquitous and fundamental to Thai religious traditions.

Spirit Houses

There are many forms of spirit in Thailand, and like everything else they are arranged into a hierarchy. Every house, building, or construction has a spirit house in or near it, to accommodate the spirits of the land that they are understood to have displaced. These spirit houses can be modest or extremely opulent, usually reflecting the status of the building and its occupants. Offerings

are made to the spirit house on a regular basis to placate the status-conscious spirits and dissuade them from causing misfortune. In rural villages, there are also larger shrines to ancestor spirits who are similarly placated when people marry or move house. These types of spirit are relatively low in the hierarchy, and as such are usually not represented with statues.

An example of a household spirit shrine.

Chinese Deities

Many Chinese religious practices have become conventional in Bangkok and elsewhere, most noticeably in the form of Chinese spirit shrines in urban locations. These are distinguished by their tiled roofs and red paint. The Chinese goddess Kuan Yin is very popular in Thailand, and her shrines and statues continue to multiply in number and size.

A wooden statue of the thousand-handed Kuan Yin at Kanchanaburi.

Royal Spirits

Historical royalty from all of the dynasties associated with the territory of present-day Thailand are worshiped as powerful, high-status guardian spirits. This is undertaken at nominally secular national monuments depicting royalty, and at other less formal statues and shrines all over the country. The popularity of different royal spirits changes according to fashion, often following the examples set by rich celebrity patrons. Throughout the country you'll see many statues of King Rama V, King Naresuan, and King Taksin, whose cults are particularly widespread.

The worship of royal spirits almost qualifies as a subreligion of its own. It overlaps with conservative nationalism and Buddhism, and is a major factor in the domestic tourist industry. Take care to behave with respect in the vicinity of any royal shrine or statue.

Supplication and Society

What is spirit worship? Spirits are supplicated generally for two reasons: to satisfy their need for acknowledgement and respect, and thus avoid the misfortune that their anger may bring about, and to enjoin them to intervene in the material world and provide assistance or blessings to individuals who need it. Supplication involves prostrating before a statue or shrine and making an initial offering of flowers and incense before making one's request. The supplicant then pledges to return with a larger thanks-offering if the request is granted. The request might concern advancement at work, exams, success in a new business venture, health matters, and so on. Some ask for winning lottery numbers, others for general blessings.

The supplication of spirits corresponds to how Thais often behave in a society that is characterized by mutually beneficial relationships (see page 23). In this setting, ostentatious displays of respect and gifts are given in exchange for favors rendered, which corresponds to how Thais are expected to behave in all sorts of personal and professional settings, in particular with regards to authority, from whom advancement may be sought for a price.

THE MONARCHY

Thailand's Civic Religion
Thailand's monarchy is quite unlike any other in the world and is much more than just an enduring ceremonial institution. While it has always been at the center of society and politics in Thailand and Siam, the monarchy and its status as it is today originated in the early reign of Rama IX, the father of the present king. A pious Buddhist and polymath trained in engineering, King Rama IX set up a range of

A portrait of King Bhumibol Adulyadej, known as Rama IX.

royal foundations and projects, and frequently toured the countryside to oversee rural development. Along with the inherently sacred nature of kingship, this beneficence was used as the basis for a very successful, media-driven cult of personality. As a result, from the 1960s onward, the visibility and prestige of the royal family increased rapidly, as did their functions and duties. The resurgence of the monarchy in Thai society occurred with the support of the Thai military and the Americans, who saw Southeast Asia as an important theater in their struggle against communism. In the later years of Rama IX's reign, his virtue was celebrated as being beyond comparison, and the institution of monarchy had permeated almost every sphere of Thai public and cultural life. While playing no formal role in government, the king became a symbol of stability, virtue, and tradition, and the monarchy a dependable institution against a backdrop of unstable governments and the uncertainties of the Cold War.

Today, royal portraits festoon almost every home, business, and office, and royal flags often fly alongside the national flag. The royal anthem, different from the national anthem, is played before every cinema showing and sports event, during which all present are expected to stand. The royal news is broadcast on all channels at around 8:00 p.m. every day, and royal birthday celebrations and official ceremonies are broadcast live on every channel. Every Thai university graduate receives their degree certificate from the king or another member of the royal family.

The worship of historical royalty has increased hand in hand with the current monarchy's prestige since the early years of Rama IX's reign. Whether considered a Buddha-to-be, a royal saint, a reincarnated Hindu god, or just a person of extreme virtue, Rama IX's statuette or picture is often found in personal shrines alongside the Buddha and other deities.

Politics, Popular Opinion, and Lèse-majesté
Despite how things appear on the surface, the monarchy has become more controversial since

around the turn of the century. This was to do with the perceived role of the institution in the events surrounding the ousting of ex-prime minister Thaksin Shinawatra in 2006, and its subsequent alignment during the ensuing political struggles that continue today.

Thailand has one of the strictest lèse-majesté laws in the world, which prohibits any public criticism of the monarchy and punishes it with a prison sentence of three to fifteen years *per charge*. Foreigners may eventually be granted royal pardon, but not before a period spent in prison. Make no mistake: even a mild or unintended gesture of disrespect can result in a very serious situation, even online. Anyone can file a complaint about lèse-majesté, and the police are obligated to investigate each one.

Many Thais love and celebrate their monarchy and are pleased and proud to see visitors doing the same. Before you try to discuss the monarchy with anyone beyond pleasantries, remember the risks and sensitivities involved. Unless you know what you're doing and who you're speaking to, it's perhaps best to avoid the subject.

The New Reign

Rama IX passed away in 2016 after a prolonged stay in hospital, after which the country went into an official period of mourning that lasted for one year. Following this, Thais bore witness to two spectacular royal ceremonies that few had ever seen before: a

King Rama X rides upon a golden palanquin during his coronation in 2019.

king's funeral and a coronation. The latter took place in May 2019, with a lavish ceremony that involved the king being anointed with sacred water from 107 holy sites in 76 provinces around Thailand.

Rama X came to the throne in very different circumstances to his father. His succession went smoothly and he has undertaken royal patronage of various projects in the spheres of education, healthcare, and agricultural development. He also presided over the creation of the *jìt asă*— a kind of royalist volunteer association. Whilst the Thai monarchy is subject to more discussion in international media than ever before, it shows little sign of losing its centrality in Thai culture anytime soon.

RELIGIOUS ETIQUETTE

Almost all religious and royal sites are accustomed to receiving tourists. They all require that you remove your shoes and dress respectfully—as mentioned, this means no vests and covering the legs to at least the knees. Bigger monasteries often have sarongs that can be borrowed at their entrances. Most monasteries are bustling places with lots of noise and activity, and you may be surprised by the lack of somberness even during rituals. While visiting a monastery, drinking water and consuming snacks is fine, smoking and drinking alcohol strictly prohibited. Royal palaces on the other hand are extremely somber, and there are often additional points of etiquette which are explained at each site. Photography is generally fine in monasteries, but usually prohibited at royal sites. If in doubt, ask.

Monks are not permitted to touch women, and so care should be taken not to get too close or brush against them accidentally. They are given priority seating on public transport, and you will be expected to stand up to accommodate them if need be. Monks are often very friendly and keen to chat to visitors, especially if they happen to speak any English. They won't expect you to behave as a Thai would, but try to be as respectful as possible and keep your head at a lower level than theirs if seated. Statues, shrines, and all representations of monks, deities, and royalty should be accorded the same respect as the real thing. Be careful when sitting in a monastery not to have your feet unwittingly pointing at a statue or a monk.

Some larger monasteries that receive many tourists charge foreigners an entrance fee, such as those in the Grand Palace complex in Bangkok or Doi Suthep Monastery in Chiang Mai. This is usually very modest, and unlike the dual pricing system in national parks, is balanced by the fact that Thai Buddhists will usually spend the same or more on offerings in the monastery.

FESTIVALS

Thailand has a rich tradition of colorful, spectacular, and sometimes bizarre festivals, some of which are not to be missed if you're a first-time visitor. While many have a religious element, a relaxed fairground atmosphere can be expected at most, and with lots of fun. Here is a description of a few Thai festivals worth knowing about:

Songkran

Songkran, the Thai New Year, began as a modest tradition that involved sprinkling lustral water on Buddha statues but today has evolved into a nationwide, three-day water fight. Held on April 13 to15, Thais will generally travel back to their hometown to be with their family for this festival, which has comparable status to

If water fights aren't your thing, it might be better to skip Thailand over Songkran.

that of Christmas in the West. Expect loud music and partying of all kind. Above all, expect to get very wet.

Bun Bang Fai (Rocket Festival)

The Rocket Festival is a Lao tradition practiced all over Laos and the northeast of Thailand. This spectacular celebration lasts for three days and includes dancing, traditional music, and parades, and finally a competition in which homemade rockets are fired into the air to encourage rainfall. The rockets can be large and elaborately ornamented objects, but it is best to be cautious and keep a bit of distance at this stage, as injuries are not uncommon. Otherwise, you can let your hair down because this is a wild and thirsty event! The Bang Fai festival takes place in Yasothon province at the beginning of May.

Masked performers take part in the Ta Kohn ghost festival in the northeastern Loei province.

Ta Khon (Ghost Festival)

A picturesque festival in which locals wear tall, specially crafted masks decorated with intricate detail. Games are played and masked processions take place over the first two days, and on the third day people assemble to listen to sermons given by monks. The origins of the festival lie in a Jataka tale about a celebration held by the followers of the Buddha that was so loud it woke the dead. The festival takes place in Dan Sai in Loei province and is held between March and July. Local spirit mediums calculate the specific dates for the festival each year, so check in advance for precise dates.

Phuket Vegetarian Festival

This festival is a riot of fireworks, processions, spirit possessions, offerings, and most notably, demonstrations from participants of their immunity to pain by walking on hot coals and nail beds, and sticking all manner of sharp and blunt objects through the cheeks. As part of the festival, participants also abstain from meat, alcohol, certain other foods, and sex for nine days. The festival usually falls between September–October and takes place on Phuket Island.

Monkey Feast

This unusual festival takes place every November at a ruined Khmer temple in the middle of Lopburi, which just happens to be overrun with macaques. While the place is worth a visit for this alone, during the festival an enormous banquet of carved fruit and vegetables is laid on for these occasionally aggressive monkeys, and the result is a photographer's treat. Keep your wits about you—macaques can open bags, remove hats and glasses, and pull things out of trouser pockets in a flash.

Loi Kratong (Lantern Festival)

This nationwide festival involves the release of elaborate flower and banana-leafed baskets into rivers, lakes, and canals. Reasons for doing this include to thank the Goddess of Water and casting off one's misdeeds for the year; sometimes you'll see people placing coins, hair, and even fingernails inside the baskets to this end. Many attend simply to enjoy the spectacle. Loi Kratong falls over two days in the twelvth month of the lunar calendar which is most

Monks let off lanterns into the night sky as part of the Loi Kratong festival celebrations.

often around November time, and is best experienced in the north, where it is accompanied by the release of paper lanterns into the night sky.

Chinese New Year

While Chinese New Year celebrations are held around the country, they are perhaps best witnessed in Yaowarat, Bangkok's labyrinthine Chinatown. Expect dancing dragons, fireworks, rows of swinging lanterns, and lots and lots of food. Many Thais in this area and indeed the rest of Bangkok have Chinese ancestry, and this is a well-attended celebration that both brings family together and marks an auspicious start to the year. This lunar festival takes place over three days around January/February time.

FESTIVAL CALENDAR

Jan 1 New Year's Day Thais send each other cards and give presents.

Jan 28–30 Trut Jin Chinese Lunar New Year

Feb* Chiang Mai Flower Festival

Apr 6 Chakri Day This day honors the present royal dynasty.

Apr 13–15 Songkran Thai Lunar New Year

May* Royal Ploughing Ceremony This day marks the traditional start of the rice growing season.

May 1 Labor Day

May 5 Coronation Day This day commemorates the enthronement of King Bhumibol in 1950 and is marked by official celebrations.

May* Bun Bang Fai Rocket Festival

July* Khao Pansa Day The start of Buddhist Lent

August 12 The Queen Mother's Birthday/ Mother's Day

Oct* Bang Fai Phaya Nak Mekong Fireball Festival

Oct 23 Chulalongkorn Day held in honor of King Rama V.

October* Tod Kathin An important day in the Buddhist calendar in which the lay community offer monks new robes.

Oct/Nov Loi Kratong Lantern Festival

Oct/Nov Phuket Vegetarian Festival

Dec 5 Rama IX's Birthday/ Father's Day

Dec 10 Constitution Day

* Exact dates for these festivals vary according to the lunar calendar

CHAPTER FOUR

MAKING FRIENDS

Thais are for the most part warm, generous, and sociable people. Whenever the opportunity arises, people will get together and go out for coffee, food, or drinks. You'll find it easy to make casual friendships in Thailand, and as a foreigner your novelty value will mean no shortage of social invitations if you are friendly and approachable. True friendship, however—one in which there is mutual trust and reliability, and which comes with expectations and obligations—takes time and effort. Meaningful friendships can be won, however, and though they won't be established overnight, they are well worth the effort. Such friendships in Thailand are highly valued and you will find Thai friends to be caring, fun-loving, and generous.

FRIENDSHIP AND FORMALITY

While casual acquaintances are easy to come by in Thailand, building sincere and long-lasting connections with people is more challenging, particularly for short-term visitors. One of the reasons for this is that Thais are raised to contain their emotions and to maintain social harmony, which is partly why they can appear so affable and easygoing. Penetrating beyond this layer and getting somebody to open up emotionally, or even to speak frankly and without levity about their opinions, can be a tall order. As such, friendships and social groupings can be decidedly "easy come, easy go" in nature.

For most Thais, enduring social circles are made up of friends made in school. The same group of friends will appear at each other's house-blessing parties, the funerals of each other's parents, and will sometimes go on short holidays together. Reunion parties and outings are also common. Socializing with work colleagues is also common, though these associations can be short-lived. Building deeper friendships later in life certainly can happen, but the development of a real sense of trust and lasting attachment between two friends is perhaps less common than it is in the West.

Social reticence can be more pronounced in relationships between people of unequal status, whether the difference is due to class, age, or financial means. If your intention is to get to know somebody well and to befriend them, then it helps be aware of the social dynamic and adjust your expectations accordingly. Don't be surprised or offended if people are not as forthcoming as you would hope.

Meeting new people in Thailand is actually very easy. For foreigners, having no Thai language can be just as much an asset as being fluent in the language—Thais who are learning English or who speak it already will always be glad of the opportunity of having a friend with whom they can practice, although they may be shy at first. If you speak some Thai most people will be delighted and charmed that you have made the effort, as so few do.

When speaking with new acquaintances any topic of conversation is fair game, although it is a good idea to avoid Thai politics and the monarchy unless your new acquaintance brings it up. After learning a few details about you and where you are from, you are likely to be asked about your impressions of the country. Thais are always very pleased to hear compliments on any aspect of their culture so there's no harm in considering what positive observations you may like to share beforehand. Personal questions about your age, work, or marital status are perfectly acceptable in Thailand, so there's no need to take offense if you find yourself being asked for these details by someone you've just met.

Once you have established a friendship, what should you expect? You will likely now be friends on Line and Facebook, the two most popular social media apps in Thailand and where most socialize on a daily if not hourly basis. Dropping in on people at home if you happen to be nearby is less common and less practical than getting in touch by Line or phone first. More usually, arrangements will be made for a group to meet in a restaurant, bar, or café. If you decline more than one of these invitations in a row you might need to initiate the next meeting yourself to reassure your friend that you're still interested. In any case, most get-togethers will be in public places, and if you are invited to someone's home or introduced to their family, it is a sign that your friendship is deepening.

GOING OUT

Thais will rarely turn down the opportunity to socialize and have fun and are normally not fussy or picky about where they go or what they do. If the group is mixed, then some formality may remain between the most senior and junior members, but you'll be surprised how little this stands in the way of a good time. In general, the more the merrier, and you shouldn't be surprised if people bring other friends with them unannounced. Thais usually enjoy being out in places with lots of other people. The more people and noise, the better. Anywhere that serves food and drink, shopping malls, cinemas, markets, fairgrounds, and even monasteries and shrines are popular places to spend at with friends. Thais are much less likely to invite people to visit them at home, partly because many people live in a single room or small apartment, where it is simply not convenient to entertain people.

While often a social group will be made up of peers, sometimes an elder or more senior person will take

precedence as such and form the center of the group, decide where to go, and, if appropriate, will also pay the bill. Though it is convention that the host or the most senior person will pay the bill, today people will just as frequently divide it among themselves. That said, it is commonly assumed that *faràng* are very well off compared to Thais and depending on the company you may sometimes be expected to pay. If you aren't sure about this, it's perfectly acceptable to ask or to be upfront about having a limited budget if that is the case.

Attitudes to alcohol, such as when, where, and with whom it is acceptable to consume it, are quite different to those in the West. Yes, Thailand is certainly a drinking country, but it is a tolerated vice that is prohibited in the Buddhist precepts, and this attitude can be invoked without warning sometimes. If unsure, follow the example of the group you're with, particularly if somebody else is paying.

CLUBS AND SOCIETIES

As we've seen, Thais are very comfortable in groups; they are used to communal living and have a much high capacity for compromise and tolerance. It is also common for people to join clubs and associations so that they can pursue their hobbies and pastimes with others. Such groups provide an important social outlet and an excuse for meals, outings, and travel. You will notice some of these groups by the identical shirts they wear when they are together.

Some of these groups are rather exclusive, such as motorcycle or scooter associations, and also those who play prestige sports together such as golf. Others are much more informal, often having their origin in a Facebook group. These are much easier to join, and some of them use English deliberately to keep their group more inclusive. If you like idea of finding a group to join, a quick online search, particularly on Facebook, will let you know what's available.

HOSPITALITY AND THE HOME

Those with the capacity to entertain guests at home usually enjoy doing so. Normally they will have a specific room or area in the house for doing this called *hông rúp kàek* ("room for receiving guests"). Thais remove their shoes before entering anyone's home, and you should too. There will usually be a rack outside for this purpose.

There is no special etiquette for guests that differs greatly from Western convention, other than perhaps being a bit less assertive in conversation and making sure to compliment your host—too much is better than not enough. It is fine to be a little late, and fine to arrive on time too. If you're stuck in traffic or delayed and will be more than twenty minutes late, a phone call will be appreciated. Bringing your host a small gift is also welcome.

When it comes to meals, the Thai convention is to pile the table with dishes and allow everyone to help themselves. You may find that as a foreigner, people take an interest in having you try as many things as possible, but beyond this there are no rules and you can eat as much or as little as you wish. Unlike in some other Asian countries, no significance is read into whether you finish all the food on your plate or not.

GIFT GIVING

Gift giving is an important part of Thai culture. If anyone goes abroad or to another province on holiday, they will always load up on souvenirs and local produce to give to family and friends back home—it is a gesture

of respect as often as affection. Giving a gift to your
dinner host, teacher, boss, or patron will also go down
well. Giving a small gift to somebody of whom you are
asking a favor or whose cooperation you are hoping to
secure can also yield positive results.

Thais always love to receive gifts from foreign
countries, especially Western ones. If you anticipate
being in a situation where gift giving would be
appropriate, bringing something from home is a good
idea. This could be chocolate, other confectionery,
as well as nationally or locally themed souvenirs.
Good-quality liquor is another popular gift, but as
above, exercise some judgment about whether this is
appropriate. There are periodic campaigns on Thai TV
discouraging the practice of giving alcohol as a gift,
though few would take offense at this.

DATING AND ROMANCE

As previously mentioned, there is no particular
cultural barrier preventing or discouraging Thais
from dating foreigners. On the contrary, there is an
entire sub-culture built around the idea consisting of
dating websites, Facebook groups, novels, exposés,
relationship guidebooks, and so on. The days when
this subject was the preserve of professional Thai
hostesses and older Western men are over, and while
this stereotype may still cast a long shadow, it is no
longer valid.

The Gift of Giving

As an ethnographer I often have to ingratiate myself with individuals in order to obtain interviews. Sometimes this is extremely difficult, especially when the person I am pursuing is of high status, has little free time, and has nothing to gain by cooperating with me. Once there was a particular woman whose insight I really needed, but who was very standoffish whenever I approached her. Upon my third attempt to secure an interview I offered her, without much thought, a gift-wrapped box of Japanese tea that somebody else had given me and I was surprised at how much this changed her attitude; I was immediately taken more seriously and found her to be much more obliging.

Meeting and dating Thais is straightforward, but there are a number of cultural differences that are worth being aware of. Public displays of affection are frowned upon no matter who they are exchanged between; anything approaching heavy petting is completely unacceptable and even holding hands is controversial. Despite the existence of more progressive attitudes, traditional gender roles endure for the most part and men will be expected to pay when going out. Women for their part may be expected to defer to men's

preferences. These kinds of issues can be approached through simple conversation but remember that Thais will generally override their own feelings to avoid conflict, especially in the case of a Thai woman and a foreign man. This can bottle up over time.

As the relationship gets more serious you will be expected to meet parents and other family members. Depending on the circumstances, you might be expected to spend considerable time with other family members, especially in the countryside where many extended families live in the same village together. Typically, Westerners in serious relationships with Thais find that they have to negotiate for time and space on their own as this is less of a priority for Thais who are more accustomed to communal living.

When arguments arise, Westerners can find it frustrating when their Thai partners do not speak openly about their needs and feelings or respond to their partner's emotional frankness in kind. Often, displeasure or anger will find expression through impenetrable silence—this should be borne with patience rather than insistence on an immediate explanation, which may only serve to make things worse.

A final word for men who fall in love and hope to marry: in nearly all cases you will be expected to pay a dowry. This can be negotiable, and in many cases after it has been ceremonially paid it is returned in part or in full to the newlyweds. Your spouse will explain the options, which vary greatly depending on region and status.

Though perhaps less common, it is just as socially acceptable for Thai men and foreign women to date. In the early stages of a relationship it might help to keep in mind that in Thailand it is conventionally men who take the lead and make decisions, but this is not set in stone and women should not be worried about being assertive.

CHAPTER FIVE

THE THAIS AT HOME

Family is central to Thai culture and society. As the most basic social unit, it is an idealized microcosm of most other forms of Thai organization and ultimately the nation as a whole. Parents and grandparents are to be revered, and can never be repaid for the gift of birth that they have bestowed—so all Thai children are taught. The family unit is healthy and well-functioning when its members respect the hierarchy and are yielding and loyal to each other, putting each other first. With no adequate state support for the elderly and impoverished, family represents an indispensable source of support for many Thais.

FAMILY SRUCTURE AND NORMS

The family unit is based on the extended rather than the nuclear family, even if the latter has begun to take prominence among the urban middle class. The hierarchical and conservative nature of this unit is deeply embedded: age dictates seniority, and authority is deferred to without question. This means that children and young adults are accustomed to parents and guardians playing a much greater role in their lives and decision-making than is usually the case in the West. Despite this, the bosom of the family is warm and children are celebrated and indulged.

Filial piety cannot be overestimated in Thailand. Many famous Thai people publish books about their parents, especially their mothers, which conventionally read like highly sentimental hagiographies. Most parents depend on their children to take care of them in old age and sending a parent or elderly relative to a care-home is unthinkable. With such an emphasis on loyalty and

obligation, nepotism is more or less a universal reality in Thailand.

The hierarchical structure of the family is reproduced in society through the use of pronouns that reflect filial relationships. Thais refer to themselves and each other as elder or younger siblings, and when speaking to somebody of their parents' generation, will call that person "aunty" or "uncle," and sometimes even "mother" or "father" depending on the context. This doesn't imply any closeness or obligation beyond simply acknowledging each other's relative status.

NAMES AND NICKNAMES

Most Thai names are derived from Pali or Sanskrit and to an outsider can seem inordinately long. Most given names are two or three syllables and surnames longer, though they are rarely used in everyday speech—many good friends do not know each other's surnames.

Indeed, surnames were only introduced in Siam in 1913. An act passed under King Rama VI required every family to register a surname in line with newly imposed census regulations. No family was supposed to have the same surname, and all surnames had to have a minimum of ten consonants, which explains their length and complexity (this rule has since been relaxed). In choosing a surname, the family would approach a monk or a Pali/Sanskrit-literate fortune teller for advice on the most auspicious syllables to use.

All Thais also have a nickname which is used in all everyday situations and remains with them for life. These are usually convenient one-syllable names and are not always complimentary: *Daeng* (Red), *Uân* (Fatty), *Òt* (Tadpole), *Mŏo* (Piggy), *Nói* (Titch, or Little One). For the most part Thais are not as sensitive as Westerners about their physical characteristics.

HOUSES AND LIVING ARRANGEMENTS

The three most common forms of living space in Thailand are houses, the shophouse terraces, and apartment blocks. Traditionally, Thai houses were made of wood and built on stilts to protect them from flooding, as well as to provide a sheltered space for any animals, equipment, and vehicles the family may own. While this style of housing persists in the countryside, in towns and cities houses are now mostly built of concrete and look decidedly Western, with only superficial nods to traditional Thai architecture.

Shophouses are found in both urban and rural settings. The ground floor comprises an open-fronted shop or workshop, with one or more stories above used for living, usually by the owners of the shop. Apartment blocks are more common in urban areas and can vary from very cheap single-room blocks to opulent condominiums with infinity pools, spas, and health clubs. The same broad spectrum applies to houses. Suburban gated housing estates are commonly found

An example of a traditionally styled Thai house, built of wood and raised on stilts.

though are much more expensive than ordinary villages and towns. Not only are the latter cheaper but they are more convenient (and less sterile too!). Many people also design and build their own houses, giving rise to a much more interesting urban texture than what gated communities offer.

Renting accommodation anywhere in Thailand is surprisingly easy, and for the moment at least, is still much cheaper than much of the West, and cheaper than in Thailand's less developed neighbors too. Living in a Thai building or neighborhood (as opposed to one catering specifically for foreigners) is entirely possible and highly recommended—it will be both cheaper in cost and richer in experience. A rental contract will usually be for between six and twelve months. In most cases you will be expected to pay one month's deposit and two months' rent up front.

DAILY LIFE

Thais are early risers. In the cities this is invariably because breakfast and commuting through rush hour gridlock can take up a sizable portion of the morning before work which usually begins at 8:00 or 9:00 a.m. In rural areas people rise early to buy or sell food at markets, prepare the day's meals, take care of animals, or otherwise begin a long list of agricultural and horticultural tasks.

Many people in the city will eat out for lunch, but some bring a packed lunch in a Thai tiffin-carrier (*bpin-dtoh*), a charming multitiered lunch box of Indian origin. Work ends at 5:00 p.m. for most people, after which it's time for a short bout of socializing and eating before getting back home. Wandering through villages anywhere in the country as the sun goes down is very pleasant. At this time most people are sitting together out in the street, eating and drinking, laughing, and listening to music or playing games. The feeling of community and relaxed well-being is infectious.

BIRTH

Until recently childbirth took place at home and was subject to a variety of taboos, folkloric prescriptions, as well as superstitions concerning the *kwăn* (see page 107) and the unwelcome attention of spirits. Now it generally takes place in hospitals and clinics with full antenatal care.

Astrology is still very much alive in Thailand and most Thais know the exact time and certainly the day that they were born. This information is used to calculate horoscopes and determine which days, colors, and objects may or may not be auspicious. As we will see with weddings, it is common for people to consult monks or astrologers for advice on the precise timing of an important undertaking.

Traditionally, one's lifespan is reckoned in cycles of twelve years and each year is named after one of twelve animals which originate in the Chinese zodiac: rat, buffalo, tiger, rabbit, dragon, snake, horse, sheep, monkey, cock, dog, and pig. The animal of the year in which you were born is believed to influence both your character and outlook.

Generally speaking, birthdays do not hold significant meaning for Thais. Gifts are appreciated but not expected, except between partners. Modest get-togethers with friends are the norm for those who want to celebrate their birthday, as is singing Happy Birthday, but many people will not mark it in any significant way. Some will use the occasion to go to a monastery to make merit.

A bride and groom gesture at the wedding ceremony. Surin province, Isan.

WEDDINGS

Marriage is both part of the glue that holds families together and the key to their survival and growth. As such it is a valued institution in Thai society. Like most other important ceremonies and rites of passage, it can vary greatly depending on where you are and the social class to which the couple belong.

For most of Thailand's history arranged marriages were the norm across all sections of Thai society, and while it may still occur in some aristocratic families, it is no longer the case for the majority. One tradition that has survived is that of the dowry, or bride-price (see page 99). Every man is expected to pay a dowry to the parents of his betrothed, and Thai banks often arrange loans to facilitate this as standard. The amount is agreed upon beforehand and ostentatiously presented on a large tray as part of the ceremony.

In all cases an astrologer will be consulted to ensure that the wedding will take place on a date and time considered to be propitious—down to the nearest minute! This is why, as you may have noticed is the case for other important events in Thailand too, wedding ceremonies are often set for extremely specific times like 11:28 a.m. or 4:53 p.m.

Other common elements of wedding ceremonies include the tying of a sacred thread around the wrists of the couple by a series of family elders. There is also usually a short procession, the arranging of betel nut and other offerings on ritual trays, and the blessing of the nuptial bed. While there is no Buddhist ceremony per se, weddings are an opportunity for plenty of merit to be made, whether through donations or inviting monks to chant at the ceremony. In rural areas permission for the union is asked of ancestor spirits who are appeased with food. Finally, to legalize the marriage, the couple must attend their nearest local government office and register it officially for a fee.

Weddings in Thailand can be held at home, in hotels and special venues, and even at the beach. They will always involve food, drink, and relaxed socializing, regardless of the social background of the couple. The only particular etiquette to be aware of is the convention to offer a gift of some money in an envelope, either by dropping it into a box near the entrance of the venue, or handing it directly to the host who you will be presented to at some point. If you are invited to the wedding of somebody rich or well connected, you'll be given a protocol sheet with your invite. Expect to have to rent appropriate clothing of a color deemed auspicious for the couple. Though originally a Western notion, honeymoons are catching on, especially among those who can afford them.

The Thai government is currently considering a bill permitting civil unions, but this has yet to be made into law at the time of writing.

Divorce in Thailand is both more common and easier to attain today than it was in the past, and the stigma once attached to getting divorced has eroded considerably in recent years.

DEATH AND FUNERALS

Unless it comes violently or prematurely, death is met with an impressive equanimity in Thailand. Displays of grief or emotion at funerals are rare. In fact, with all the food and entertainment involved they sometimes better resemble temple fairs.

As with weddings, funerary rites in Thailand vary from region to region, but all will include the following: the ritual bathing of the corpse and the display of the coffin in which it is kept for several days at the home of the deceased, various public merit-making ceremonies on behalf of the deceased, the relocation of the coffin to a monastery where monks perform chants over an evening or longer, and finally, the cremation of the corpse at an outdoor crematorium.

In addition to location, the kind of funeral held will depend on the status of the deceased. The family is expected to make appropriate donations to the monastery, as well as to provide meals and entertainment for at least three days. This ranges from monks giving sermons and performing sections of the Jataka tales, to loud music, food, and even karaoke.

The funeral is an opportunity for the family to both generate merit for the deceased and to maintain face in having done so sufficiently, so the more people who attend the better. Funerals facilitate the ritualized reenactment of the social hierarchy, and so higher-status guests are invited to take pride of place and display their patronage through merit-making and even just by being there.

The immense cost of funerals is mitigated somewhat by donations from guests, who offer these in an envelope inscribed with their name. The size of the donation, anything from 20 baht and beyond (sometimes much further beyond), reflects the donor's means and status, as well as how close they were to the deceased or their family.

If you need to attend a funeral, it is appropriate to dress in black. You might be invited to attend any or all parts of the public ceremony, all of which will require no more of you than lighting some incense near the coffin as you enter, and offering a polite *wai* to anyone you are introduced to. Drinking and gambling into the night were once common at funerals, but government campaigns have largely put a stop to this.

GENDER AND SEXUALITY

When it comes to the position of women, Thailand is relatively progressive compared to other East and Southeast Asian countries. On the surface, however, things are still very conservative: women are expected to defer to their husbands' preferences in all matters, assume the role of housewives, with all the household responsibilities that entails, and raise the children. The traditional idea that men and women have distinct and separate roles in life persists. However, women are more mobile than it would seem. Many have careers in trade, business, and the civil service, and, though they are underrepresented in politics, Thailand has had a female prime minister. The managerial ranks of all sectors are still dominated by men though. Socially, the traditional image of Thai women as being entirely demure and deferential is misleading. Today, many are just as outgoing, curious, and independent as men may happen to be, and do not appreciate the assumption that this might be otherwise.

One interesting taboo that does endure concerns menstrual blood. This is believed to be a very potent substance with magical properties that can negatively affect male prowess. For this reason, you will rarely see female undergarments hanging with other laundry, and many women will abstain from a range of activities and behavior while they are menstruating.

As for men, fewer today feel the pressure to conform to masculine identity norms which are conservative and macho in nature. These norms can mostly be observed within certain professional milieu, for example the police and the army, and in some business circles.

Thailand's attitude to gay and transgender rights is progressive and the country is a very friendly one for LGBT visitors, who will meet little if any discrimination. Bangkok in particular has a famously open, vibrant, and extensive gay scene. For LGBT Thais there is still some stigma that can affect job opportunities, and same-sex couples do not receive the same legal rights that heterosexual couples do. In 2019 parliamentary discussions began with a view to further equalizing their standing.

Transgender women are very common in Thailand. Known in Thai as *kàtoey*, they are free to assert their identity from a young age, sometimes even before high school, and in general draw no censure or special attention in Thai society. *Katoeys* are by no means confined to performing in "ladyboy" cabaret shows that you may come across in tourist districts; rather they live throughout the country and are employed in every sector, from retail clerk to civil servant, just like everyone else. The term *kàtoey* can also sometimes refer to homosexual men more broadly.

CHAPTER SIX

TIME OUT

From quaint to cosmopolitan, rustic to elegant, traditional to the downright bizarre, Thailand, and Bangkok in particular, is overflowing with food and entertainment to suit every taste. This is no idle observation and it's partly what makes Thailand such a popular destination for tourists and expatriates of all kinds. Relatively speaking, the cost of living in the country has risen considerably in recent years, but those on more limited budgets are still spoilt for choice, especially if they are willing to be a little open-minded and explore.

EATING OUT—THAI STYLE

Thais enjoy eating out, and while those of greater means may hold dinner parties at home, it is far more common for Thais to invite each other to a restaurant. Everywhere you go in Thailand you will

A family enjoy an evening meal on Yoawarat Road in Bangkok's lively Chinatown district.

find a diversity of quality restaurants and street stalls serving up the fresh and fragrant dishes that have brought Thailand's cuisine such renown.

Restaurant dining is an informal activity in Thailand and it is normal to have a variety of dishes spread out on the table for everyone to pick and choose from. There is no need to stand on ceremony—when the food arrives everyone digs in. Fork and spoon are the usual implements of choice, and chopsticks for noodles.

As a rule, whoever makes the invitation will pay for everyone, and if it's your turn to pick up the bill, *chek bin dûai kúp/kâ* is how you ask the waiter for the check.

TIPPING

In Western-style hotels a service charge is normally added to the bill; in other places it is taken for granted that a tip is included in the price, but you may leave a small tip if you wish. The same applies to taxis.

In addition to Thai food, cuisines of all types are available, including European, American, Israeli and Middle Eastern, Chinese, Indian, Japanese, and many more. In Bangkok there are whole neighborhoods that cater to specific national cuisines and culture, including Korea-town, a Japanese district, the Western-orientated traveler ghetto of Khao San Road and its environs, and a spectacular vintage Chinatown. Restaurants of every type and size are represented, from noodle shacks by the side of the road to grand, purpose-built facilities with live entertainment.

THAI CUISINE

Thailand's cuisine is much more diverse and sophisticated than what is usually found in Thai restaurants abroad. In the main it is characterized by its use of fresh ingredients and strong, aromatic flavors. While it is quintessentially Southeast Asian in this regard, it has also absorbed a great deal of influence through the ingredients and cooking styles of India, China, and the West.

Indigenous Thai food has four basic categories: *dtôm* (boiled), *yum* (spicy hot salads), *dtum* (salads or pastes pounded in a mortar), and *gaeng* (curries). Fried dishes of Chinese influence are also ubiquitous. Within Thailand there are at least four distinct regional cuisines: Central, Isan, Northern/Lanna, and Southern. More on each of the cuisines is discussed below.

Food in Thai is *ahǎn*, and a restaurant is referred to as *rán ahǎn* (food shop). While restaurants in the main centers are used to catering to foreigners, in smaller towns many are not, and the unsuspecting gourmet who chooses an interesting-looking dish from the counter may find it alarmingly fiery unless they ask for it to

A vendor prepares noodles on the water at the Damnoen Saduak floating market, Bangkok.

be served otherwise. It is somewhat ironic that Thai cuisine is associated in the West with fiery chili peppers, as the capsicum was first introduced to the region from the Americas by the Portuguese in the 17th century. It is now an omnipresent element in Thai food, although many Thais themselves do not like overly hot dishes and will make their preference clear when ordering in a restaurant. The best remedy for burning chilis on the tongue is yoghurt or other dairy products.

To help you avoid any unwanted surprises you may find the following expressions useful. Note the untranslatable politeness particles used at the end of the sentences; these are used in any short exchange with a stranger. *Kúp* is used by male speakers, and *kâ* by female speakers.

HOT OR NOT

What is this?: *nêe arai kúp/kâ*
Is it spicy?: *pèt mái, kúp/kâ*
No, it isn't: *mâi pèt kúp/kâ*
Yes, it is spicy: *pèt, kúp/kâ*
It's a little spicy: *pèt nít nòi*
It's very spicy: *pèt mâk*
Please make it less spicy: *mâi dtông pèt mâk kúp/kâ*
Don't add any chillis: *mâi sài prík*

For an explanation of pronunciation markings, see page 183.

Midday diners enjoy a quick lunch at a popular roadside food stall.

MEALS AND RESTAURANTS

Many Thais like to start their day with either rice soup (*kâo dtôm*) or porridge (*jòk*), and meals throughout the day will consist of a combination of meat or fish, often both together, and vegetable dishes accompanied with either rice or noodles. Desserts are optional but are more common in a formal dinner setting. Western breakfasts, continental or English/American, are also popular with some Thais and are easy to find in cities and tourist areas across Thailand. In almost all cases, Thai food is considerably cheaper than Western alternatives, and often much healthier too!

Restaurants that specialize in a particular regional cuisine are usually more expensive and can be found serving food throughout the day. Eateries that sell Hainanese noodle soup (*gŏo-ay dtǐew*) and single-dish meals like fried rice (*ahăn dtam sùng*) often shut at around 2:00 p.m. after the lunch rush. Both of these breakfast/lunch options are cheap and often excellent. Hainanese noodle soup is comfort food for Thais, and for some expats too, once they master how to order it. Few noodle shops have English menus, but don't let this put you off. The staff will be very helpful if you have a basic grasp of what you want to communicate. You need to order the type of noodle (small: *sên lék*, flat: *sên yài*, egg: *sên mee*), the broth (clear: *nám săi*, tom yum: *dtôm yum*, or *nám dtòk* – a kind of blood sauce), and finally whatever meat option the shop offers, such as chicken, pork or beef (*gai, mŏo* or *néu-a*).

Single dish restaurants often do have an English menu or at least one with pictures, and they will always have vegetarian options. Their menu always includes Pad Thai, fried rice, fried noodles, fried vegetables, and a choice of curries with the usual range of meat and seafood options.

WORDS ON THE MENU

The most common words on the Thai menu include *kài* (egg), *gài* (chicken), *mŏo* (pork), *néu-a* (beef), and *bpèt* (duck). Dried beef and pork have a particularly strong flavor.

Thailand is particularly renowned for its fish and seafood dishes, though if you are dining some distance from the sea, bear in mind that river fish might be fresher. Popular seafood includes *gôong* (prawn), *bpla* (fish), *bpla kàpong* (sea bass, a great favorite), *bpla mùek* (squid), *hŏi* (shellfish), *hŏi kreng* (cockles), *ahăn taley* (mixed seafood), and *bpoo* (crab).

Among the vegetables you will find *hŏm* (onion), *hèt* (mushroom), *pakàd* (lettuce), *makĕu-atêt* (tomatoes), and *mun faràng* (potatoes).

TYPICAL DISHES

Thai dishes use all the ingredients specified above, to which they add various flavors, notably *gatiem* (garlic), *pàk chee* (coriander), *prík tai* (black pepper), *dtakrái* (lemongrass), *kĭng* (ginger), and *prík* (chili). Here are some of the most common dishes:

Gaeng pèt (curry), and *gaeng pèt gài* (chicken curry). You may need to differentiate between *gaeng kĭew wăn* (green curry) and *gaeng pèt deng* (red curry). *Gaeng massuman* will be a mild and fragrant curry common n the south of Thailand.

Gaeng jèut is a clear pork and vegetable broth with no spice or heat. *Gaeng jèut néu-a* is beef soup.

Dtôm yum is a hot, spicy soup. This is one of the most popular dishes in Thailand, especially *dtôm yum gûng* (spicy prawn soup).

Kâo pùt (fried rice) is a popular one-dish meal, and can be served with almost anything. *Kâo pùt mŏo* is pork-fried rice. Cucumber and spring onions usually accompany the dish.

Kwítiǎu (noodle soup) is of Chinese origin and found on many a noodle stall. It is sometimes eaten with chopsticks. *Bami* are noodles and come in various shapes and sizes. *Bami lad na gûng* is prawn cooked with noodles and is a meal in itself. *Meekrob* (crispy noodles) is also well worth trying.

Tâwt mun bpla or tâwt mun koong (fish or prawn cakes) are interesting, chewy dishes.

Yum (salad) is much spicier than in the West.

Kâo soo-ǎy (plain rice) is usually steamed, delightfully fluffy, and of high quality. This is the staple food of Thailand and is eaten with virtually every meal. *Kâo nǐew* (sticky rice) is a specialty of the northeast, where it is sometimes cooked in banana leaves.

The following words are useful: *nèung* (steamed), *yâng* (grilled), *pùt* (fried), *tâwt* (deep fried), *prîew-wǎn* (sweet and sour). When ordering, make sure you put the ingredient first and the manner of preparation second, so you get *gôong tâwt* (fried prawn), *pla príuwǎn* (sweet and sour fish).

If you have a food allergy, ask a Thai friend to write down the information for you in Thai so that you can communicate it clearly when eating out.

REGIONAL CUISINES

Bangkok/Central

The cuisine of the central plains uses jasmine rice as its staple and features a lot of curries and broths made with coconut milk. Most of the dishes found in Thai restaurants in the West are Central cuisine, as they are considered the most accessible and also the most cosmopolitan.

South
Southern cuisine similarly includes a lot of curries and coconut milk but tends to be much spicier. It has been influenced by Indian, Malay, and Indonesian cooking, in addition to Hainanese and Cantonese cuisines from the north. Located between the South China and Andaman Seas, Southern cuisine uses a great deal of fresh seafood. Those who struggle with spicy food can try the milder *kâo yum*, a tossed salad of rice, herbs, and vegetables.

Isan
Sharing many characteristics with the cuisine of neighboring Laos, Isan food is both highly distinctive and

delicious, though some consider it low class "peasant" food. The staple is glutinous or sticky rice eaten with the fingers. A range of spicy salads accompany this, including *lâb* (minced chicken/pork/fish with red onion, herbs, and spices, uniquely flavored with powdered, toasted rice) and the classic dish *sôm dtum* (chopped unripe papaya with string beans, tomato, peanuts, and dried prawns in lime and sugar palm dressing). *Sôm dtum* is a must-try and goes best with sticky rice and grilled chicken. It is usually served with a lot of chili, so be sure to tell your waiter if you want a milder version.

Northern/Lanna

As in Isan, sticky rice, spicy pounded salads, and pastes are the staples of northern cuisine. Uniquely, it has also absorbed elements of Burmese/Shan cuisine such as fermented relishes and robust curries. Signature dishes include *kâo soi* (mild yellow curry with egg noodles and chicken) and *sâi oo-a* (a very distinctive spicy sausage, and highly recommended). Don't miss the fragrant *dtum makěu-a* (smoked eggplant paste) and the other striking relishes that northerners enjoy as an accompaniment to rice.

CONDIMENTS

To the Western palate, Thai food is boldly flavored and thoroughly seasoned. However, Thais will also usually make use of additional condiments without restraint, including various combinations of chili, vinegar, soy sauce, and even cane sugar. Most fundamental is *nám pla*, a thin brown sauce made from salted fish that has been allowed to ferment. It smells potent, but is very tasty when used sparingly. In restaurants it is often found in a ceramic bowl with chopped chilis and fresh garlic.

FRUITS AND DESSERTS

Thailand has a wonderful variety of fruit (*pŏnlamaí*) including a number of exotic varieties that seldom appear in shops back home. Fresh fruit is available everywhere and changes with the seasons. There are ubiquitous stalls and carts on the street that sell fruit ready peeled and prepared, or head to any fresh produce market to buy your fruit unprepared and in greater quantity.

Do not be put off by oranges with green skins: that is their natural color when ripe. You will find bananas (*gloo-ây*), different kinds of mangos (*mamûang*), papayas (*malagor*), pineapples (*sùbpárót*), watermelon (*dtaeng moh*), pomelo (*sôm-oh*), rambutan (*ngo*), custard apple (*nói na*), jackfruit (*kanŏon*), guava (*faràng*), dragon fruit (*gâew mungon*), rose apples (*chompoo*), lychee (*linjee*), longan (*lum-yài*), and mangosteen (*mungkòot*). Strawberries, apples, and other temperate climate fruit are now being cultivated in the north of Thailand.

Coconut (*mapráo*) can be bought fresh from food stands. The vendor will chop the top off and give you a straw so you can drink the juice.

Thai desserts (*kanŏm*) tend to be rather sweet, and often contain rice or coconut. Among the most common ones are *kanŏm mapráo* (coconut cake), *gloo-ây bùat chee* (banana in coconut cream), *gloo-ây tâwt* (banana fritters), and *săngkayă fúktong* (pumpkin custard). Many other locally distinct confectionaries are available from vendors and at markets.

The great luxury for Thais is *durian*, which is a large, spiky, pithy fruit that has an overpowering odor, but is treasured for its flavor. If you can't stand the smell then settle for *durian* ice cream instead—though you may find your bravery well rewarded in this case.

DRINKS

Non-Alcoholic Beverages

Thais drink a lot of tea and there have been tea plantations in the north for decades. Thais particularly enjoy *cha tai,* a sweetened tea with condensed milk that is made fresh and sold everywhere, in addition to various herbal iced teas (*námcha yen*). Sugary sodas are also popular, but Thais are just as likely to drink water with their meals, or alcohol.

Western-style coffee shops are now omnipresent throughout the country, and most do a very good cup of Thai-grown coffee. Robusta is grown in the south and arabica in the north, Doi Tung and Doi Chang being internationally recognized examples of the latter. Akha Ama Coffee do some excellent roasts and are worth looking out for.

Lots of shops and vendors sell fruit smoothies and freshly squeezed juices, and a range of purified and mineral bottled waters are available everywhere.

Alcoholic Beverages

Thailand traditionally had a rich culture of uniquely flavored medicinal alcoholic drinks, but this is unfortunately almost dead due to corporate monopolies and the laws that operate in their favor. Alcohol is also very highly taxed in Thailand, meaning costs, particularly of imported alcohols, are prohibitive. Despite this, interest in artisanal and crafted libations is running high.

Beer

Beer production in Thailand was until recently limited to two dominating companies who produce the popular domestic lager brands Singha, Leo, and Chang. In 2016, however, the craft beer scene took off dramatically when small brewers began working around stringent policies that had previously held them back by brewing beer abroad in order to import and sell it back in Thailand. Now there are craft beer bars all over the country, including in pretty far-flung locations. Regular restaurants too are beginning to stock a wider range of beers to meet the growing demand. Craft beers from other Southeast Asian countries are also available. The downside is that they are all hideously expensive, usually between 200–300 baht per glass (this is partly due to the heavy taxes and partly because the culture surrounding it is somewhat exclusive, a bit like wine used to be twenty or more years ago). There are exceptions and the craft beer scene is exciting and well attended despite the cost; with any luck it will continue to grow as more brewers emerge.

Spirits
Imported spirits are widely available and, as above, are expensive. Thais rarely take spirits neat, and even a rare single malt whisky will be diluted with ice and soda. A variety of local spirits are distilled which are much cheaper. *Sangsom* is a locally produced sugarcane rum that is particularly popular with tourists and locals alike.

Wine
Again, imported wine is extremely expensive and is considered a luxury, although Thailand now has its own vineyards in the north and northeast. Chateau de Loei from the northern province of Loei is one of the longest established, and Maejo Red from the Agricultural University at Chiang Mai also has its admirers. Local wines are also made from other fruit, such as mangosteen.

WHEN DRINKING

Cheers: *chôk dee*
Glass: *gâew*
Bottle: kùat
"One more bottle": *kǒ èek nèung kùat*
Cup or bowl: *too-ây*
Plate: *jan*
Milk: *nom*
"Without milk": *mâi sài nom*
Sugar: *nám dtan*

SHOPPING

You can buy virtually anything in Bangkok, often at bargain-basement prices. Imports, including foods, tend to be expensive, but there are now many local alternatives and cheaper options alongside big name and artisan brands.

Thailand's industrial base has expanded enormously in the past forty years, and the country now has a network of factories producing electrical goods, textiles, pharmaceuticals, and so on. If you want to go on a shopping spree you will find most of these local products reasonably priced and of good quality.

Bargaining is unavoidable in Thailand, to the pleasure of some and the chagrin of others. Sometimes foreigners become angry when their attempts at securing a discount are rejected, but this may be because they are in a commercial space where prices are fixed, such as big brand-

CAVEAT EMPTOR

Buyer beware! Every year visitors are conned into buying *objets d'art* they believe to be genuine, but which are not. At archaeological sites like Ayutthaya, for instance, people will approach you offering to sell you genuine antiques that will have been made last week and skillfully aged. A genuine antique is likely to be expensive, and if you plan to take it out of the country, you may well need to procure an export license.

Fake designer goods and pirated films and software are available everywhere in Bangkok and other urban centers. Every so often the police crack down on this, but it persists. Needless to say, quality is not guaranteed.

You need to exercise particular care when buying jewelry, especially when approached in the street. Reputable dealers do not solicit in this way, nor do they organize special promotions. All claims as to the value of the object need to be verified carefully, and if you have any doubts as to the reliability of a jewelry dealer you should check with the Tourist Assistance Center of the Tourist Authority of Thailand. The Tourist Authority Web site is www.tat.or.th.

name and chain retail stores, supermarkets in malls, and fresh produce markets. (Fresh food is generally sold at fixed prices everywhere.) Souvenirs, clothing, and goods at places such as the Weekend Market at Chaktuchak can be bargained for. Note that when you buy things like electronic goods in high street stores, you'll often be given something extra for free as part of the deal. Ask if this is the case by saying "*tăem arai mái (kúp/kâ)*."

Siam Square and its surrounds, Pratunam, and Sukhumvit areas have perhaps the widest range of shops, but you have good shopping facilities in most areas of Bangkok, including the major business area around Silom and Suriwong. Bobae Tower is the place to go for buying clothes in bulk. There are many well-stocked and spectacular markets, including picturesque floating markets such as those at Taling Chan and Amphawa.

In the provinces you will also find a wide range of goods on sale, even in the smallest townships. Most of the large hotels and tourist centers have souvenir shops selling Thai handicrafts. Thai silk, bronzeware, lacquerware, Celadon pottery, and wood carvings are among the most attractive items.

CULTURAL LIFE

Classical Culture

Thailand has a rich and multilayered culture that draws both from Indian and Southeast Asian traditions. One of the fundamental components in the classical sphere of this culture, apart from Buddhism, is the Indian literary epic the Ramayana, rendered as the Ramakien in Thai. The latter was composed in Sanskrit probably between the seventh and fourth centuries BCE, and tells the

A traditional *lakhon* dancer performs the Ramayana, known in Thai as Ramakien.

story of Prince Rama, whose wife is kidnapped by the demon king Ravana, provoking a great war which Rama wins before returning home to be crowned king. The *Ramakien* had deep political and religious significance in the royal court, providing an ideal model for kingship and inspired a range of motifs and symbols used in royal rituals and ceremonies, some of which can still be seen today. Today the epic is most identifiable in classical dance, theater, and art.

If you are interested in classical culture, then some contextual knowledge will be helpful. The bookshop at Silpakorn Fine Arts University has an excellent range of literature on this subject, and if you would like to engage a guide or go on a guided tour the Tourist Authority of Thailand (TAT)—www.tourismthailand.org—can help. The following descriptions offer a brief introduction to various classical art forms.

Thai Dance

Thai classical dance (*lakhon*) was originally performed only at the royal court, but it can now be seen in theaters (notably the National Theater) and is often performed at wedding parties and other celebrations, as well as in restaurants that cater to tourists.

The whole of the Ramakien would take days to perform, and a performance normally consists of just one episode. A chorus and narrators recite the narrative with musical accompaniment. The dancers tell the story through the use of stylized gestures and postures, and their movements are very slow. They hold their bodies straight from the neck to the hips and move them up and down with knees bent, stretching to the rhythm of the music. Their brocaded costumes resemble traditional royal dress and that of literary and mythological figures. Finely crafted masks—sacred objects that are also sometimes used in spirit possession ceremonies—are also worn.

Classical Music

Thai classical music uses a tonal system that is different from Western music, but those who are acquainted with Indonesian gamelan music will find many similarities. Unlike Western music which has full tones and semitones in the octave, Thai music has an eight-note octave consisting of full tones. Southeast Asian classical music is truly *sui generis*, and its cacophonous harmonies are a very special pleasure to behold if you get the chance to see it live. It nearly died out in the twentieth century but was revitalized by the American musician Bruce Gaston and the Thai *ranat* player Bunyong KetKhong, whose playing was described by Chinese Premier Zhou Enlai as "the sound of pearls falling on a jade plate."

Among the instruments used are:
- The *ranat*, or Thai xylophone, which is usually slightly curved and resembles a boat.
- Drums (*glong*) come in a variety of shapes and sizes; the shallow drum is known as the *ram mana*.

- The *kawng* is a gong; one common variation is the *kawng wong yai*, which is a series of gongs (*kong*) suspended on a circular frame.
- The *saw* is a stringed instrument that is played with a bow. Its body is made from half a coconut shell.
- The *ching* are cymbals.
- The bamboo pipe (*pee*) is a type of oboe.
- The orchestra that accompanies Thai classical dance performances—known as a *piphat* orchestra—usually includes a *ranad, pee, ching, kawng wong yai*, and a *glong*.

Sculpture and Architecture

Just as Western art is categorized by various styles and periods, so too is the art of Thailand, most notably in regard to the style of Buddha images and statues. While this system of classification is itself antiquated and historically questionable, for the purposes of orientation it helps to have a basic knowledge of it.

In the Dvaravati period (sixth to the twelfth centuries CE) the statues have a broad face and well-formed features. In the southern Srivijaya period (seventh to thirteenth centuries) the features are well proportioned and show more direct Indian influences. The Lopburi style is interpreted as more gentle and benign. Statues from the Sukothai period (thirteenth to fourteenth centuries) are notable for their undulating forms, graceful curves, and oval faces. This period and style is celebrated as the Golden Age of Thai culture, and the style is much reproduced in popular art today. Buddha images from the U Thong or Early Ayutthaya periods (fourteenth century) have squarish faces, thick lips, and smiling mouths. It is at this point that the Dvaravati, Khmer, and Sukhothai styles are thought to have merged. During the Ayutthaya period (fifteenth to eighteenth centuries) there is a move away from the simplicity of the earlier styles and the figures become much more ornate. The Rattanakosin style (late eighteenth century onward) is the style associated with the Chakri dynasty.

Most statues, regardless of style, will have the following characteristics derived from a list found in the Pali Canon: a protuberance on the top of the skull; spiral curls; distended earlobes; arms long enough to enable him to touch his knees without stooping; flat foot soles; and projecting heels.

Although the Buddha is normally represented in the sitting position, he is also depicted in standing, walking, and reclining postures; the latter shows the Buddha entering Nirvana. There are a number of different hand gestures that usually depict meditation, calling the earth to witness, teaching, and dispelling fear. In some cases, the Buddha is seated on a lotus flower, in others inside a coiled *naga* serpent, a reminder of how the Hindu god of the underworld saved the Buddha from drowning as he was meditating.

Wat Benchamabopit in Bangkok, popularly known as the Marble Temple, has a cloister containing fifty-two

A Buddha statue at Wat Si Chum, part of the ruins at the UNESCO World Heritage site at Sukothai.

Buddha images assembled in the reign of Rama V, that were intended to display examples from all of these styles.

Classical architecture is primarily monastic and palatial. Up until late last century, ruins and material heritage were not valued in Thai culture in the way that they are in the West. This means that very little survives from these earlier periods because, once a site was abandoned, the masonry was often removed and recycled elsewhere. You can see heavily reconstructed ruins in the UNESCO-inscribed historical parks of Ayutthaya, Sukothai, Sri Satchanalai, and Kampaeng Phet. Other smaller ruin complexes proliferate throughout the country. Unfortunately, neither culture nor climate has been kind to other types of vintage architecture. The dilapidated but fascinating Mahakan Fort community in Bangkok was the oldest surviving example of its kind, until its residents lost a long struggle with the government and were evicted in 2018. The old houses have since been demolished to make way for a park.

POPULAR CULTURE

Popular Theater (*likay*)
Troupes of players perform all over the country, often at temple fairs. The actors improvise the dialogue, lyrics, and plot of the play making great use of puns and topical allusions. Music is provided by a type of mouth organ (*ken*) consisting of fourteen pieces of cane or bamboo.

Cinema

There are cinemas all over the country and Thais love going to see films. Thailand has a thriving film industry and frequently hosts Hollywood and other Asian productions for location filming. In the late 1990s the so-called Thai New Wave emerged in the form of directors Nonzee Nimibutr, Pen-Ek Ratanaruang, and Wisit Sasanatieng. Their films were more artistic and experimental and had an impact outside the country too, receiving critical attention and international distribution. Good examples are Nonzee's *Nang Nak*, and Wisit's singular and entertaining *Tears of the Black Tiger*. Perhaps the most remarkable artist and filmmaker working in Thailand today is Apichatpong Weerasethakul, whose films have quite rightly received international acclaim and won multiple prizes at the Cannes Film Festival, most notably in 2010 with *Uncle Boonmee Who Can Recall His Past Lives*. He is, in fact, a lot more popular outside his homeland than in it, where his films have been censored and criticized by the authorities on a number of occasions for presenting Thai culture and institutions in a potentially negative light.

Popular Music

Trends in Thai pop music have run broadly parallel to those in the West up to the present day, with some exceptions. In the 1970s a kind of protest folk rock movement emerged called *plaeng pêu-a chiwít*, or "Songs for Life," which gave birth to many popular bands. One such band, Carabao, are still widely listened to, though their music is less political today. A genre of Thai popular music from Isan called *lûk tûng,* or "Children of the Field," is still very popular and can be heard on taxi radios and in karaoke bars all over the country. Today, young Thais are very keen on K-pop and similar electronic dance acts from abroad.

Popular Dance

At celebrations it's quite usual for people to take to the dance floor and sway to the beat of the music, gesturing gracefully with their hands. This dance is called the *ramwong* and is enjoyed in Thailand, Cambodia, and Laos. Thais are very pleased if foreign visitors join in, however rudimentary their dancing skills. Other kinds of equally graceful folk dances are practiced in different regions in addition to the *ramwong*, often at spirit possession ceremonies and other seasonal festivals. If you have the chance, these are colorful events and well worth attending.

SPORTS

Thai Boxing (*muay thai*)

Thai boxing is a standing combat sport in which any part of the body can be used to strike, except the head. Knockouts are usually the result of blows from elbows and knees rather than fists or feet. It is more or less Thailand's national sport, and is now internationally popular, with many fighters from around the world

coming to Thailand to train. There are training gyms and stadiums all over the country, but the two main venues for televised fights are Lumpini and Rachadamneon in Bangkok.

Martial Arts (*krabi krabong*)

A number of other martial arts are practiced in Thailand which use swords, staffs, clubs, and halberds (a two-handed pole axe). Demonstrations can be seen in theme parks and restaurants around the country. These are much less popular than boxing, however.

Cockfighting

Cockfighting is extremely popular in Thailand. It is heavily regulated for the reason that it is one of the few sports upon which Thais are permitted to legally gamble. Naturally, there is a rich underground cockfighting culture which adds to the generally illicit feel that the sport carries with it. Because of this, it can take some effort to find and attend a bout as a foreign spectator. If it's a gory spectacle you're after you might be disappointed; bouts are not always as violent as you might imagine. For novelty's sake, have a look in any Thai newsagent at the huge range of cockfighting magazines with their "Cock of the Month" pull-outs. Thais also rear fighting fish, beetles, and buffaloes.

Kite Flying

This is a popular pastime in the hot season, as is kite fighting in which a "male" kite (*chula*) sets out to ensnare a "female" kite (*pukpao*). The principle venue for this is Sanam Luang in front of the Grand Palace in Bangkok.

Takraw

This game involves keeping a woven rattan ball in the air without using one's hands and can be seen being played by groups of young men up and down the country. A variation on this has rules similar to basketball.

Other more familiar sports that are popular in Thailand include soccer, rugby, horse racing, and golf, the latter two being relatively exclusive and elite pastimes. There are two racecourses in Bangkok—the Royal Turf Club and the Royal Bangkok Sports Club, and various golf courses around the country.

NIGHTLIFE

Thai nightlife is incredible and a lot more diverse than it used to be, with bars, pubs, restaurants, and clubs to suit all tastes. The country's reputation for men-only entertainment is well earned, but today this scene is generally either hidden from view or confined within special zones. Make no mistake, Thai nightlife is accessible to anyone and everyone, and it's almost impossible not to have an adventure.

Bangkok has all the entertainment that you would expect to find in a cosmopolitan center, including music venues and theater, jazz bars, rooftop restaurants, art galleries, and traditional performances of music or dance. Seaside resorts have entertainment for foreign tourists ranging from cabaret to the notorious full-moon dance parties on the beach. A glance at the Friday editions of the Bangkok English-language newspapers will give you some idea as to what is going on. Chiang Mai, Hua Hin, Pattaya, and Phuket have weekly English-language papers that give prominence to entertainment in the immediate vicinity. Shutting times vary throughout the country and are subject to constant revision. Locals can tell you what the situation is, and where the after-hours places are hidden.

THE SEX INDUSTRY

The estimated number of sex workers in Thailand runs anywhere between 150–300,000. Contrary to what some people assume, the vast majority of these represent the domestic market, and not those in the sex tourism industry. Domestically orientated prostitution takes a variety of forms, primarily "bath and massage" parlours and karaoke bars. The oldest trade in the world has long been a part of Thai society and culture; today it is officially illegal and unofficially tolerated.

The side of the industry that is seen by most foreigners is that which is aimed specifically at them and has its origin in American R&R zones that existed during the Vietnam War. Today it is found in certain areas of Bangkok, Pattaya, and elsewhere, and comprise hostess bars, go-go bars, and clubs, all of which are staffed overwhelmingly by girls who have migrated from other provinces. Many tourist areas also have smaller concentrations of hostess bars. In some areas, such as the notorious Patpong in Bangkok, the sex industry has become a parody of itself, with expensive "ping-pong" shows aimed at curious gawking tourists of both sexes, most of whom have no intention of actually hiring a prostitute. Other zones like Nana Plaza and Soi Cowboy cater to Western expatriates and tourists but are today bounded enclaves subject to increasingly strict regulation. Broadly speaking, the industry appears to be contracting, and declined rapidly during the 2020 coronavirus pandemic.

The sex industry will always be a controversial and divisive subject, and it is difficult to come across informed, neutral, and sober observations from either side of the aisle. It's impossible to deny the darker elements below the surface, and no matter how happy and well-adjusted hostesses may appear drinking and cavorting in bars, almost all of them ended up there as a result of social and economic pressure, compromise, and a grinding lack of alternatives. Having said that, relative to sex workers elsewhere, they have a much greater degree of independence and much less obligation. They certainly lead a very different and more socially and physically mobile existence compared to their peers employed in factories and other sectors. This perceived freedom and the possibility of much more money to send home to parents can make working in a bar a tempting option.

Most hostess bars are welcoming to all, and there is no implied obligation upon the male visitor to do anything other than drink, chat, and play bar games (expect to lose heavily at Connect-4). Hostesses make some or all of their money from drinks bought for them by customers, which are sold at a high price and referred to as "lady drinks." It is convention to buy a hostess a drink if you wish her to sit and talk with you for more than a few minutes.

TWO WARNINGS

Prostitution

Thailand was remarkably successful at combating its AIDS epidemic in the 1990s, but needless to say, HIV and other STDs are still a serious risk for prostitutes and their customers. If you do have sex, use a condom. The Thai word for condom is *tŏong yang*, and they are widely available from chemists and the ubiquitous 7-11. Sex with minors, or prostitutes under the age of 18, is illegal and punished accordingly.

Drugs

Drug laws in Thailand are extremely harsh, and the possession of even small amounts of contraband can potentially result in a long prison sentence. Foreigners receive no special treatment; in fact, they are usually made an example of. The laws are enforced by police to differing degrees depending on where you are in the country and according to personal luck, but make no mistake: the risk you take in buying and using illegal drugs in Thailand is profoundly greater than in most Western countries.

CHAPTER SEVEN

TRAVEL, HEALTH, & SAFETY

EASE OF TRAVEL

Another aspect of Thailand's appeal is the ease with which one can travel around the country, including to its furthest and least tamed corners. The country has good transportation infrastructure with well-maintained roads and a well-developed public transportation network. Accommodation is excellent and plentiful in the main centers, and the hotels that are available in smaller towns are more than adequate. There is no need to "rough it" unless you really want to.

With so many millions migrating to Bangkok and elsewhere for work, Thais are very used to traveling and are enthusiastic tourists in their own country. Most monasteries, resorts, national parks, and other attractions have large photogenic signs somewhere prominent so Thais can "check in" on Facebook, which they love to do. The domestic tourism industry is actually much larger than the international one in terms of numbers.

Traveling by bus or train is much cheaper and often just as convenient as services aimed exclusively at foreign tourists. You'll find most Thais friendly and helpful, and usually a minimum of English is spoken. There are now ATMs throughout the country, but it's always a good idea to keep plenty of Thai currency in low denomination notes, especially when traveling in the provinces.

ARRIVAL

Most visitors to Bangkok arrive at Suvarnabhumi Airport which replaced Don Muang as the country's primary international airport in 2007. Approximately 18 miles (30 km) east of the city center, it boasts a vast four-story terminal building, 139.12 acres (563,000 sq. m) in area. Before the 2020 coronavirus pandemic, the airport handled around sixty million passengers a year, making it Asia's eleventh-busiest airport. The arrivals area is on Level 2 and you need to proceed down to Level 1 for transport into Bangkok and elsewhere. In addition to taxis and airport limousines, there is a new high-speed rail link that will whisk you into central Bangkok in around twenty minutes. Bangkok's former international airport, Don Muang, to the north of the city, is used by the low-cost carrier Air Asia, Nok Air, and other domestic airlines.

There are direct international flights to some of the provincial airports, notably Chiang Mai and Phuket, which eliminate the need to change planes in Bangkok. If you come to Bangkok on the international express train from Malaysia, the terminus is Hualampong Railway Station which is in the middle of Bangkok and where you can connect to Bangkok's efficient MRT subway.

VISAS

Visitors of most nationalities are offered a "Visa Exemption Stamp" upon arrival, which allows for thirty consecutive days of travel inside the country. If your country is not on the list, or if you plan to stay for longer than thirty days, or to work in Thailand, then you must apply for a visa at a Thai Embassy or Consulate before arrival. A tourist visa allows for up to sixty days travel and can be extended for another thirty days. Work and study visas are available, as are specific visas for those who are married to a Thai national.

The visa situation is much less flexible than it used to be, meaning that if you want to stay in Thailand for longer than six months you will have to jump through some bureaucratic hoops. The rules are enforced differently in different parts of the country and are subject to sudden and seemingly arbitrary change. For this reason, always refer to the Ministry of Foreign Affairs Web site or else the forums at Thaivisa.com, which are constantly updated and are a very useful source of visa-related information provided by knowledgeable, if occasionally choleric, expatriates.

The BTS Skytrain ferries commuters above Bangkok's busy streets.

TRANSPORTATION IN BANGKOK

Bangkok's roads are tremendously congested and it may take much longer to get to your destination than you expect. Luckily, there are multiple ways to get around, and once you are used to them, moving around the city can be easy and fun. Whatever form of public transportation you are on, there will always be seats reserved for monks and lay people are expected to give up their seats when there is no other space available. See page 194 for the best apps to download for transport and journey planning in Thailand.

Skytrain and Subway

The Skytrain (BTS) is a cheap, comfortable, and efficient way to get around central Bangkok, although it can be pretty hectic during rush hour. Several BTS stations connect with subway stations allowing for an easy interchange between lines, and routes are being extended. Maps can be found in all stations as well as on the back of your ticket.

Buses

Bangkok has an extensive bus service served by various kinds of vehicle. The cheapest of these has no air-con and open windows that let all the fumes in. If your journey is a short one, then this is by far the cheapest way to travel. All buses have a conductor, usually a woman, who will come and collect your fare. English is rarely spoken; just say the name of

your destination and she'll indicate the cost of a ticket. Have small denominations ready as conductors can't change big bills. If you want the conductor to tell you when you've arrived, say *bòk doo-ây kúp/kâ* when you're paying for the ticket.

Taxis

Bangkok's taxis are obliged to use a standardized meter which start at 35 baht, and to accept all customers regardless of destination. In reality, though most will turn on the meter if you ask, always make sure they are willing to do this before getting in—it is quite common to have to hail three or four cars before you find a driver who will accept your fare. One reason for this is because many drivers wish to remain in a particular district of the city; venturing further may mean getting stuck in serious traffic without a passenger.

Unfortunately, some drivers attempt to apply made-up surcharges especially for their foreign passengers, all of which should be swiftly refused. However, it is convention that the passenger always pays the express tollway fee. Grab is the go-to hail-a-ride app for taxis in Thailand and is safe and reliable. For those new to Bangkok, using the app insulates against arbitrary price hikes by some municipal taxi drivers, and removes potential confusion about your destination.

Tuk-tuks are traditionally cheaper than taxis, but these days their drivers will rarely offer tourists a fair price. They are aware of the novel and iconic nature of their vehicles and in many cases would rather drive off and find someone more gullible than concede to your attempts to bargain them back down to something approaching reasonable. Conversely, if you are offered a suspiciously low price, this probably means the driver intends to take you to a shop or hotel who pays him a commission for doing so, whether you want to go there or not. In addition to this, tuk-tuks are as vulnerable to traffic jams as cars, are entirely exposed to the relentless exhaust fumes of surrounding traffic, and if you are tall, completely obstruct your view with their roof covering.

Motorcycle taxis are a very useful means of getting about. Journeys can be hair-raising, but they can move through solid traffic more or less unimpeded. Moto-taxi drivers are recognizable by their orange waistcoats which identify which taxi group they belong to and which district they work in. You'll often see the drivers sitting together beside the road. Thais use them for

Moto taxi drivers in orange high-vis jackets wait for passengers to whisk away.

short journeys of ten minutes or less. Routes have a set fare which is often printed on vinyl near where the drivers are sat. If you want one to take you further, the price must be negotiated.

Water Transportation

Travel on Bangkok's waterways is another cheap and reliable way to move around the city. It is also the most pleasant and provides a breezy vantage point from which to survey and explore the city. There is a riverboat service on the Chao Phraya that links up with various Skytrain stations and other popular locations, as well as an extensive canal boat service, which will take you through an otherworldly network of precariously dangling, canal-side slum architecture throughout the

A passenger ferry on the Khlong Saen Saep canal, Bangkok.

older and newer districts of Bangkok. Marvel at how the
ticket collectors communicate with the driver through
a repertoire of special whistles. Passengers know which
route they are on by the colour of the flag the boat flies,
and a black flag means it is the last boat of the day,
usually at around 7:00 p.m. There is also a tourist-only
boat service which services the most popular tourist
sites (identified by a blue flag) though this is more
expensive. Most ordinary service tickets on the river
and canals are between 10 to 30 baht.

Car Rental

There are several good local car rental companies in
Bangkok that offer more competitive rates than the
multinationals. You may prefer to hire a driver with the

car, which will add only about 50 percent to the cost. Driving is on the left—as in the UK and Australia—and although there is a Highway Code of sorts, most drivers appear to ignore it. Be prepared to drive aggressively and let your motto be "Who dares, wins." Be prepared to spend considerable amounts of time sitting in traffic.

Motorcycles are also available for rent and on a more informal basis. There is less facility for this in Bangkok than there is in the rest of the country, however.

Walking

Many parts of the city reward the patient and curious walker, and if Bangkok is new to you, depending on the district, the sights, smells, and sounds can be intoxicating. Thanks to the city's proficient network of public transport, one needn't worry about going too far or getting lost. The heat, humidity, and traffic can be intense, however, so go slowly, stay hydrated and keep your eyes open.

TRANSPORTATION IN THE PROVINCES

Air

A number of airlines operate scheduled services to provincial airports from Bangkok, including Thai Airways, Air Asia, Bangkok Air, and Nok Air. If you are in a hurry to get around, this is your transportation of choice.

Train

This is a good, and safe, way to see the country. Train services run from Bangkok to Chiang Mai, Nong Kai (where you can catch a shuttle train to Laos) and Ubon in the northeast, Aranyaprathet in the east, Kanchanaburi in the west, and via Hat Yai in the south to Kuala Lumpur and Singapore. There are three classes of travel, and there are overnight trains with sleepers (bookable in advance) on some long-distance routes. Supplements are payable for certain trains, sleepers, and air-conditioning. Charges are listed on the Thai Railways Web site (www.railway.co.th).

The Burma Railway in Kanchanaburi—also known as the Death Railway for the heavy human toll of its construction.

Most of the Thai railway system is single-track and the trains tend to amble—no Japanese-style bullet trains here yet, despite long-standing government plans to introduce them. Diesel railcars, which tend to be third-class only and with limited legroom, can be faster than the so-called express trains.

Bus

This is the cheapest way to travel between provinces. The state BKS bus company (known as "Baw Kaw Saw") runs long-distance orange buses to all parts of the country from the four bus terminals in Bangkok.

Air-conditioned long-distance buses run to some towns, and local tour companies run bus services to resorts that can pick you up at your hotel. Both of these options are more expensive. For very long journeys, such as Bangkok to Chiang Mai, bus travel is not recommended; train and air travel are more comfortable. In each province local bus companies ply short-distance routes, though buses can be uncomfortable.

There are also informal minibus services that run from Bangkok to the surrounding provinces. These can be claustrophobic as they are usually full, and their drivers are known for their aggressive driving.

Taxis

In provincial towns you will find taxis to hire, but in the smaller towns pedicabs and motorized tuk-tuks (*săm-lor*) are often a better bet, but you need to negotiate the fare in advance. Out of town you may find shared taxis (*sông-tâew*) a convenient way of getting around. These are usually small pickup trucks with seats in the back that ply regular routes and are fairly frequent. Though usually cheap, be aware that these sometimes try to charge tourists inflated prices, especially in Chiang Mai, where they are known as "red-cars."

Water Transportation
Motorized long-tailed boats operate along the extensive canal network of the central plain and the rivers.

Driving Yourself
This is a good way of getting around as Thailand has an excellent network of well-maintained main roads, some of them expressways, and traffic jams are rare in the provinces. If renting a car, make sure the rental charge includes insurance—Thai driving is erratic and many drivers seem to be oblivious to other traffic on the road. Foreign drivers are supposed to obtain a Thai license, but an international one will usually suffice. Gasoline is only lightly taxed and therefore remarkably cheap by European standards.

Thailand, especially the north, offers spectacular opportunities for motorcyclists, and it is a fine way to see the country. Bikes of all sizes can be rented in most urban centers, whether you are planning a daytrip or a regional tour.

Be aware that the roads are particularly dangerous during holiday periods, especially over the Songkran festival in April when public transportation is overstretched and the roads jam-packed. The number of road accidents is known to soar during this period.

It is common for police to set up checkpoints in urban downtown areas. They are looking for unlicensed drivers, drunk drivers, motorcyclists without helmets, out-of-date tax disks, and so on. If you are found guilty of any of these infractions, you will either be given a ticket with a fine which you must pay at a police station, or you will be asked to pay on the spot. If caught drunk driving after dark, you'll potentially face a night in lock-up and a formal charge unless you're willing to pay a very, very large fee then and there.

WHERE TO STAY

Travelers in Bangkok, Chiang Mai, and the other larger provincial capitals are completely spoilt for choice, with hotels, resorts, and guesthouses to suit every budget, and virtually every town in the country has at least one or two small hotels. It is advisable to book accommodation in advance if you are traveling during the high season. Web sites like Agoda.com and Booking.com will give you an idea of what's available.

Airbnb is very popular in Thailand, especially in Bangkok. It is however illegal, due to a law which requires all accommodation services to record the details of their foreign guests and submit them to authorities. Whether it is down to tolerance or simply the impossibility of enforcing this law, Airbnb rentals seem to operate with no problems at the present time.

SAFETY AND HAZARDS

Overall Thailand is a remarkably safe country and compares very favorably with many Western countries in this regard. Having said that, crime does occur, and the usual precautions should be taken. For example, when in crowded areas make sure your money and personal possessions are secure, and don't leave luggage unattended, even if you see others doing so.

Women traveling on their own should take care at night, particularly when walking back to their accommodation in the early hours. When out at bars or clubs, don't leave your drink unattended. Incidents of drink spiking are statistically rare, but they do happen. It is also a good idea to make sure doors and windows are secured at night as thefts have been known to occur even when there are people at home. Should you need them, the English-speaking tourist police can be reached by dialing 1155.

Scammers are a problem, especially in Bangkok, but are easily identified by their over-friendly or obsequious manner. If you are approached by a stranger and invited to go somewhere with them, the chances are it is a scam. These often involve escorting you to a gem shop or other kind of business and manipulating you into parting with your money. Others involve betting games that are rigged— gambling is illegal in Thailand and you'll have no recourse if you fall victim to this. Scams aimed at those buying or using drugs also exist, and police regularly stop and search tourists near bars and clubs late at night in Bangkok.

The law requires foreigners to carry their passport at all times, but this is rarely enforced. Carrying a photocopy of the ID page and entry stamp is a good idea, however.

HEALTH MATTERS

There are no major health concerns regarding travel in Thailand, but you should always check with your doctor and familiarize yourself with the official government health advice before setting off. If you have never traveled to an equatorial country before, there may be some vaccinations or booster shots that you will need. Malaria and other mosquito-borne diseases can be a threat, especially in some border areas, though a DEET-based lotion or spray will keep you as safe from bites as you'll ever be. Always use mosquito screens and nets at night.

It takes most people a while to physically adjust to a new environment and new cuisine, and traveler's diarrhea is a common complaint. This is managed by drinking plenty of water, practicing good hygiene, and using a medicine like Imodium if need be. If diarrhea is accompanied by a fever or other symptoms or lasts for more than a few days, then you should seek medical help.

If you are from a country with a temperate climate, Thailand's equatorial heat and humidity can also take some getting used to. Drink plenty of water and take care to stay hydrated, especially if you are drinking alcohol. Keep yourself protected from the sun with a hat and sunglasses, especially around noon time when the sun is strongest. If you start to feel unusually fatigued, take a sachet of rehydration solution or add some salt and sugar to your water. In general, you should take things slowly while you adapt.

Thailand has excellent medical care and now attracts medical tourists from all over the world. Well-stocked pharmacies abound, where you can find local and international remedies for most common ailments. If need be, you can head to straight to a hospital where you'll usually be seen by a doctor, usually only after a short wait. Make sure you obtain suitable medical and travel insurance before you arrive in the country.

CHAPTER EIGHT

BUSINESS BRIEFING

Thailand boasts the second largest economy in Southeast Asia after Indonesia with a Gross Domestic Product in excess of US $543 billion. Its free market economy and favorable business climate attract plenty of foreign investment despite political instability, and it is a regional center for international travel and trade. Exports represent two thirds of Thailand's GDP, with both services and manufacturing playing major roles. The agricultural sector, once Thailand's largest, today only accounts for 8.4 percent of GDP, though it remains a substantial employer, employing over 30 percent of Thailand's workforce.

The Thai economy has sustained a number of significant blows in its recent history, including the financial crisis of 1997, various natural disasters, and of course the global 2020 coronavirus pandemic, the long-term effects of which will be with us for some time. However, the country's economy has proved to be resilient and Thailand remains open to investment.

PREPARATION IS VITAL

While the overwhelming majority of visitors to Thailand come as tourists, an appreciable number come for professional reasons: to sell, to invest, to set up a business, to offer aid, to advise, to write about the country, to lecture, and so on. If you fall into this category you arrive with certain objectives in mind, and you naturally hope that your efforts will be successful.

Success cannot always be guaranteed. Some visitors fail spectacularly to achieve their aims and retire frustrated from the fray, blaming the Thais for being uncooperative, impossible, and closed to new ideas. Yet most of the blame probably lies not with the Thais but with the way the visitors have conducted themselves; they have not taken into account local attitudes and customs and have failed to adapt accordingly.

Nearly every foreigner arriving in Thailand suffers from a built-in disadvantage. The Thais you will meet will know more about you and the way you operate than you do about them. If you want to find out who's who in the Premier Division of UK football, you cannot do better than ask a Thai.

A surprisingly large number of Thais, especially the younger generation, will have studied abroad—in the USA, Australia, New Zealand, Europe, and elsewhere in Asia. But that does not mean that they have abandoned their own values and way of life in favor of foreign lifestyles and attitudes.

There is no excuse for arriving in Thailand in a state of ignorance, especially since there are a number of organizations that can offer you advice. Several countries have a chamber of commerce in Bangkok, and if you are a prospective investor there are a number of government and private Web sites offering information, such as www.boi.or.th. Do not overlook the various briefing organizations in your own country that can advise you on how to proceed.

MANAGEMENT THAI STYLE

If you are dealing with Thai companies or have set up a company in Thailand, do not assume that these companies are run in the same way that they would be back home. In the West people work for a company or organization, and their loyalty is to that organization. In Thailand organizations are not run collectively, as in Japan, but by one person. That person has to be someone able to exercise authority and who can command respect. The older and more important he or she is, the more they will be respected. Thai workers are loyal to their boss, provided they do all that is required of them.

However, a manager's role is not confined to achieving work targets. It spills over into other areas. In Thai society superiors have obligations to the people in their charge. They are expected to treat them kindly, paying attention to their welfare, and sometimes covering up their mistakes. A manager is often regarded as a patron by his staff and is expected to assist them in all kinds of ways, from helping their relatives find jobs to presiding over weddings.

This entails performing a balancing act between the exercise of authority and patronage. If you look after your staff well, you will earn their respect and loyalty, and they will be prepared to go that extra mile for you when you need it. But if you fail to develop a deep and trusting relationship with your subordinates, your position is weakened.

In Western companies it is usual practice to fire staff if they are not performing well. Not so in Thai companies. To dismiss someone for incompetence or laziness is a very, very last resort in Thai corporate culture. If you need to reprove someone, tread carefully. Praise is a far more potent motivator than blame.

Some international companies with subsidiaries operating in Thailand have been known to bite the bullet and fire the local manager, but actions like this can have unintended, and unfortunate, consequences.

ESTABLISHING TRUST

Thais prefer to do business with someone they know and trust, so your priority must be to establish a good working relationship. This inevitably takes time, so patience is essential. Nobody should expect to arrive in Bangkok one day and leave with a contract signed, sealed, and delivered the next.

First impressions are important, which is why you should abide strictly by the dress code, especially in Bangkok. You might imagine that in view of the capital's hot and sticky climate people would dress down for comfort, but you would be wrong. Thais dress formally for meetings or business engagements of any kind.

To make life bearable you might want to invest at the outset in a custom-made lightweight suit, which a local Indian or Chinese tailor should be able to run up for you in twenty-four hours as you recover from jet lag. Bear in mind, too, that all buildings you will be visiting have superefficient air-conditioning.

For informal gatherings outside business hours more casual attire is often worn, provided it looks smart. Brightly colored Thai cotton or silk shirts go over very well on these occasions, but it is wise to check what the dress code will be to avoid embarrassment. Special attention to grooming and hygiene is essential.

Do not underestimate the importance of social gatherings, as this is one way of gaining trust. Also, while eating your noodles you may well learn useful snippets of information that do not come out during the formal meetings. Thais who are inhibited about voicing their opinions in formal meetings because of their lack of fluency in English are more likely to open up in a more relaxed atmosphere.

So be prepared to brush up your social skills and realize that time spent making small talk in good company is often time well spent. However, avoid becoming so relaxed that you forget the rules of etiquette; steer away from taboo subjects, and don't make jokes that are liable to be lost in translation. Remember that a certain amount of flattery always goes over well.

MEETINGS

Some visitors set themselves a tight schedule on the assumption that they can cram in several meetings in one day. In Bangkok, where most meetings are likely to take place, this is frankly unrealistic. If the meetings are at different locations, you will have to allow plenty of time to get from one place to the next. Furthermore, the meetings will take longer than you expect if you are working through an interpreter.

Another factor you need to consider is the timing of a meeting. A twelve o'clock meeting is definitely out, as this is when the Thais stop for lunch. In government offices officials start leaving before the end of the afternoon. Don't be surprised if a rendezvous at 8:30 a.m. is suggested, since this is when many people arrive at their desks. While Thai attitudes to timekeeping can be maddeningly inconsistent, your punctuality will always be noted and appreciated.

Meetings tend to be formal affairs involving a number of people, though some of them will say very little. Brainstorming sessions seldom work as the Thais have been brought up in an educational tradition where one is discouraged from speaking out. The fear of being wrong or having to assume blame will usually outweigh a desire to impress with creativity or innovation. Even if they have a sound idea, junior staff may prefer not to air it in public out of deference to their superiors.

They will listen respectfully to what you have to say and there may be some pauses for interpretation and for discussion. People will smile and nod as if in agreement—though you should not assume that they do see eye to eye—and the meeting may be terminated without coming to any conclusion. This is not necessarily a bad omen.

It is important to look for clues as to the identity of the key player or decision-maker during the meeting, particularly if this is not made clear from the start. It is likely to be an older rather than a younger person, since in Thailand organizations tend to be hierarchical. Sometimes this is not always obvious, as another member of the staff may handle much of the discussion while his boss looks on.

You may get a clue from the business card you are given at the outset, which will detail a person's rank and title. Meetings usually start off with an exchange of business cards, and you should always have a good stock of your own at hand, which indicate your qualifications and your status within your organization.

If you are still not clear as to who the decision-maker is, observe the body language carefully. The others will treat him (it is usually a man) with deference, and they will always agree with his pronouncements. Harmony is always maintained in meetings. If someone enters the room they will look toward him and either *wai* or stoop.

Even if the meeting is conducted in a relaxed manner, do not assume that you can forget the rules of Thai etiquette. You need to be polite, speak in a quiet voice, and not get too animated or worked up. In other words, be cool, calm, and collected—and do your best to avoid committing any faux pas.

DEALING WITH THE GOVERNMENT

Senior government officials have a high status in Thai society, and should always be treated with a measure of deference. But bear in mind that many of the people in the top jobs will be political appointees who will often delegate decisions to permanent civil servants. These are the people of real significance, and it is important to forge as strong a relationship as possible with them since their cooperation will be crucial.

The government often calls in consultants and other experts to offer advice on a short-term basis—even though it has a highly educated cadre of civil servants who are only too aware of what needs to be done. Unfortunately, because of the hierarchical nature of the civil service, younger civil servants tend not to voice their opinions for fear of antagonizing others further up the chain of command. Promotion depends on the extent to which you toe the line, though this may no longer be true of every branch of government.

A foreign consultant starts with a built-in advantage. People in authority are more likely to listen to his or her views, even if they eventually decide not to take the advice offered. But the expert is sometimes hampered by a lack of local knowledge. Management theories that work well elsewhere may be nonstarters in Thailand because of the very different culture that operates.

The best plan is to arrive without preconceived notions and to begin by soliciting the views of people who are close to the action. If their status is fairly junior, they may never have been asked their views by their superiors. The place to hear their ideas is not in the large set-piece meetings where they will tend to keep quiet, but at a more informal level—over a coffee or a meal, for instance.

Often their ideas may prove useful, and you may well be able to incorporate them into the report without incurring any resentment. They will be flattered that you have found their suggestions worthwhile and pleased that they form part of your recommendations.

Thai civil servants are not particularly well paid, and often have second jobs. Do not expect them to work unpaid overtime in order to help you.

THE FOREIGN EXPERT

Not all consultants are so highly regarded. A British businessman was in a meeting at a government ministry with a group of Thais and one lone Westerner who seemed rather quiet and ill at ease. The businessman felt he ought to draw this fellow Westerner into the discussion and began to address some remarks to him—at which the chairman of the meeting interjected, "Don't worry about him. He's only our expert."

WOMEN IN BUSINESS

The fact that Thailand has had a woman prime minister is perhaps evidence that there are no glass ceilings in Thailand, though men still outnumber women in senior and managerial positions. There are many well qualified and competent women in business and government, and though some may appear demure and deferential, you underestimate their influence or ability at your peril.

KICKBACKS

Corruption is endemic in many parts of Southeast Asia, and Thailand is not immune to such practices, though it is by no means the worst offender.

One question that preoccupies many a newcomer is whether one should be prepared to grease any palms in order to achieve one's objectives. It is difficult to provide a satisfactory answer. As a foreigner you will not be expected to understand the nuances and extreme sensitivities in the etiquette of these sorts of situations. Attempts to be proactive on your part will almost always be interpreted as offensive, in addition to any legal implications that you may or may not be aware of.

The best solution is to find a reputable agent who can handle any payments that need to be made. Every organization operating in Thailand—whether local or foreign—has its own Mr., Mrs., or Miss Fixit who has good contacts and knows exactly what to do to make the wheels run smoothly.

The problem of corruption is regularly under Thai media spotlight, and the National Anti-Corruption Commission is kept busy, despite the apparent untouchability of many rich and powerful individuals.

One reassuring piece of advice comes from a former British Ambassador to Thailand. "You should also know that some of the most successful Western firms in Bangkok have never ever resorted to illegal payments precisely because there are so many legal ways in which these delicate matters can be resolved to everyone's mutual satisfaction."

EMPLOYMENT IN THAILAND

Opportunities for English speakers outside of business or academia in Thailand boil down to teaching English as a foreign language, although it is also possible to find work as a diving instructor in the southern islands. While all manner of unofficial arrangements are still to be found quite easily, relative to just ten years ago it is now much harder to become a legally employed teacher in Thailand. Generally, most schools will ask for a degree and a TEFL certificate at the minimum and will be suspicious if you have no experience. As with most things in Thailand, however, if you are determined, resourceful, and more interested in experience than money, you'll likely find a way. The longstanding Web site www.ajarn.com is a valuable introduction to the trade and its culture, and also includes job listings.

The visa and work permit system has also become much more rigid and demanding recently, continuing a trend that has been gaining momentum since 2006 or so. The regulations and requirements change frequently, and also depend heavily on your personal circumstances and location, so it is essential to do a lot of research online beforehand. In addition to the above Web site, the forums at www.thaivisa.com have detailed and reliable information for all parts of the country, and are constantly updated.

CHAPTER NINE

COMMUNICATING

Thais like to talk and are generally not reserved. You'll find many who are as curious about you as you may be about them. Some lack confidence but will soon relax if you are calm and polite. Thai is not as difficult to learn as you might think and if you can learn enough to bargain and have simple conversations, you'll go down extremely well, especially with those who can't or don't want to speak English.

THE THAI LANGUAGE

Thai is a tonal language with its own writing system and is spoken throughout the country (it is also generally understood in Laos, too). Just as English has absorbed influence from Latin and Greek, so too has Thai from the ancient languages of Pali and Sanskrit. New words in Thai are often derived from these languages, when they are not borrowed from English.

Like those of its neighboring countries, the Thai writing system is derived from old Khmer, which itself comes from ancient Indian scripts. The alphabet consists of forty-four characters that represent twenty-one consonant sounds, sixteen diacritical marks (which tell the reader how a letter should be pronounced) that can combine to represent thirty-two vowel sounds, and four tone markers. These vowel and tone markers can appear above, below, or on either side of a consonant character. In total there are five different tones in Thai, and the tone the speaker uses dictates the meaning of the word.

Thai is an analytic language, meaning that word order and particles do the job that inflections do in English. At a basic level, this actually makes Thai somewhat easier to learn. For instance, Thai nouns do not have plurals, pronouns may be omitted, and tense is not normally indicated. The sentence "*bpai tiew*" (go out) could mean "He has gone out," "I am going out," "She will go out," and so on, depending entirely on the context.

Learning basic Thai is not as arduous as you might expect—it requires effort as all languages do, but it is far from impossible and is well worth the effort! One difficulty for the beginner is that there is no universally used transliteration system to put Thai into roman characters, meaning that transliterated Thai words are often spelt inconsistently. For example, your guidebook may say "Kaosan Road" whilst the street sign may say "Khao San Road." In this book we transliterate the Thai alphabet with a view to as much phonetic accuracy as possible.

Consonants

ก (g)	ซ (s)	ณ (n)	ป (bp)	ร (r)	ฬ (l)
ข (k)	ฌ (ch)	ด (d)	ผ (p)	ฤ (r)	อ (o/aw)
ค (k)	ญ (y)	ต (dt)	ฝ (f)	ล (l)	ฮ (h)
ฆ (k)	ฎ (d)	ถ (t)	พ (p)	ว (w)	
ง (ng)	ฏ (dt)	ท (t)	ฟ (f)	ศ (s)	
จ (j)	ฐ (t)	ธ (t)	ภ (p)	ษ (s)	
ฉ (ch)	ฑ (t)	น (n)	ม (m)	ส (s)	
ช (ch)	ฒ (t)	บ (b)	ย (y)	ห (h)	

Vowels

Thai vowels may be short or long. As mentioned, their markers are not always placed after consonants as in English but may be placed before, above, or below, or on either side of a consonant. Here are the most common ones with their approximate pronunciation: ˘ indicates a short vowel; ˉ a long vowel.

ะ (ŭ)	ํา (ŭm)	ื (eu)	ุ (ōo)	โ (ō)
ั (ă)	ิ (ĭ)	ื (eu)	เ (ē)	ไ (ai)
า (ā)	ี (ēe)	ุ (ŏo)	แ (æ)	ใ (ai)

Tones

A further complication for English speakers is that Thai (like Chinese and Vietnamese) is a tonal language, which means that vowels are differentiated by both sound and tone. The word /kao/, for example, can mean a number of different things—rice, white, he, news, mountain, etc.—depending on the vowel tone and length. There is no need to "sing" the tones, the inflection you apply is relative your own natural speaking voice. Try listening to a Thai pronouncing them first, so you get an idea of what they sound like.

- high (often represented in transcriptions by the diacritic / ´ /)
- low / ` /
- rising / ˇ /
- falling / ˆ /
- mid—no accent or letter

A good way of practicing the tones is to recite the Thai numerals, which have low, rising, and falling tones. These are listed below.

Thai Numerals

Although Thais usually use Arabic (Western) numerals to express dates, they occasionally have recourse to their own system of numbers too:

o	(zero)	๖	(6)
๑	(1)	๗	(7)
๒	(2)	๘	(8)
๓	(3)	๙	(9)
๔	(4)	๑o	(10)
๕	(5)	๒o	(20)

Pronunciation

Certain consonants change their sound at the end of a word. The consonants l and r are pronounced n; hence the Thai tendency to pronounce "hotel" as "hoten." The sounds "j," "s," and "ch," are pronounced as "t."

COMMUNICATING WITH THAIS

Although pupils spend years learning English at school, the overall standard of spoken English of many school leavers is poor. You might have some difficulty understanding Thais, particularly in remoter areas, and they will have problems understanding you. Even in the popular tourist centers where English is widely spoken communication difficulties can arise, so be aware that what you've said may not have been entirely understood.

If your interlocutor shows a puzzled expression, try using simpler English or speaking more slowly—though not too slowly—and without any intonation. When using taxis or buses it is a good idea to get someone to write down your destination for you; failing that, write it down yourself in English. The same goes for any serious food allergies. Thais often read English more easily than they speak it.

Mixed Messages

A visiting American academic was invited to give a lecture in Bangkok. He summoned a taxi and told the driver his destination. The driver beamed at him, and a few minutes later stopped outside a massage parlor, much to the lecturer's astonishment. He had asked to be driven to Thammasart (the university). The driver thought he had said "To massage!"

UNDERSTANDING THAI ENGLISH

Most Thais who have learned English in Thailand speak the language with a very strong Thai accent. You can prime for this by expecting the following tendencies.

Thais often separate consonants by inserting a vowel between them: "whiskey" becomes "wisiki," and smart becomes "semart." Sometimes they drop a consonant: "excuse me" becomes "sku me."

As mentioned, some consonant endings are difficult for Thais to pronounce. For example, for words ending in "l" the final consonant is often pronounced "n," so you'll hear "bin" for "bill" and "Hoten Orienten" for Hotel Oriental. In words ending in the sounds "s," "ch," "j," and "th" the final consonant is pronounced "t." Sandwich becomes "senwit," "wash" becomes "wot," and Smith becomes "Samit." "R" is often pronounced as "l," as in "collect" instead of "correct," "light" instead of "right," or may be omitted altogether.

Many Thais know more English than they care to let on but are hesitant to speak it for fear of making mistakes. If a Thai is speaking to you in English, listening attentively and patiently will help the speaker to become more relaxed.

ADDRESSING PEOPLE

Thai speakers will usually add a prefix to someone's name when addressing them. These prefixes are either familial or formal. When formally addressing people of either sex the safest way is to preface their first name by *koon* ("*oo*" pronounced like the "oo" in "book"). So you would address Chuan Vongsiri as *koon* Chuan. Thais may call you by your first name in English—Mr. Bill— rather than by your surname Mr. Smith.

USEFUL EXPRESSIONS

Thank you: *kòp koon kúp/kâ*

Yes: *châi*

No: *mâi châi*

Excuse me/Sorry: *kǎw tôht*

I don't understand: *mâi kâo jai*

Good luck: *chôk dee*

Nevermind/Not to worry: *mâi bpen rai*

What is this?: *nêe aria*

How much?: *tâo rai*

Can you offer a discount?: *lót nòi dâi mái*

If a person has a royal title (and if you are on an official visit you may well meet such a person) find out in advance how to address him or her. In some cases you will be presented with a card giving all the relevant details. However, it is perfectly in order to address a person, even the prime minister, as *koon*.

In order to make any sentence polite, Thais will end it with the particles *krúp* (commonly pronounced *kúp*) or *kâ*, the first used by men and the second by women. These particles should be used universally with all greetings and formalities, so more or less anything you say can be finished with them. For example, the Thai greeting *sawat dee* becomes *sawat dee kúp* if the speaker is a man, and *sawat dee kâ* if the speaker is a woman.

LEARNING THAI

There are many advantages to being able to speak Thai, even at a rudimentary level. For one thing the Thais will appreciate your making the effort, even if they giggle at your pronunciation. Moreover, some knowledge of the language will help you to bargain more effectively in shops and at markets, and to find your way around. You may be able to get by with English in the main centers, but things can get more difficult once off the beaten track.

Pronunciation Matters

In an upcountry restaurant not far from Bangkok, an Englishman decided to order sea bass (*bpla gàpong*), looking forward with relish to this Thai specialty. Unfortunately, his pronunciation was slightly awry, and instead of a dish of delicious fish steamed in ginger and herbs he was served with a plate of sardines. The waitress had thought he wanted tinned fish (*bpla gràbpong*).

If you are planning to stay in Thailand for any length of time then learning basic Thai is highly recommended. Many choose to rely on Romanized Thai and to skip learning to read and write as they believe it will be too difficult. In reality, learning the script is a relatively easy and fun exercise, and it will result in better pronunciation and comprehension from the start.

In Thailand, the day is divided up into nine parts. Thais also use the 24-hour clock in addition to their own, but it is helpful to have an idea of the latter:

Midnight: *tîang keun*

1am – 5am: *dti nèung – dti hâ*

6am – 11am: *hòk mong cháo – sìp-èt mong cháo*

Midday: *tîang wun*

1pm: *bai mong*

2pm – 3pm: *bai sŏng mong – bai săm mong*

4pm – 6pm: *sèe mong yen – hòk mong yen*

7pm: *tôom nèung*

8pm – 11pm: *sŏng tôom – hâ tôom*

Minutes (*natee*) are put after the hour, so ten past one is *bai mong sip*. Half past midnight is tiang keun kreung (*kreung* = half).

DOS AND DON'TS

The purpose of this book has been to enable you to interpret Thai behavior from an understanding of the cultural values that motivate it, and to give you a feel for what constitutes appropriate behavior in the Land of Smiles. The following list is designed to remind you of the more important features of Thai etiquette and ensure that your relations with people remain cordial and trouble-free.

Do
- Avoid close physical contact.
- Dress smartly and conservatively.
- Flatter and praise.
- Keep your cool.
- Show respect for the institutions of monarchy and Buddhism (including monks), and for all national symbols such as the flag.
- Smile and be patient.
- Speak gently and clearly when talking in English.
- Take off your shoes when entering a house or temple.
- Use first names, preceded by *koon*.

Don't
- Don't be sarcastic.
- Don't moan or criticize.
- Don't gesticulate wildly.
- Don't get visibly annoyed.
- Don't point at people.

- Don't point with your feet or put them up when you're sitting down.
- Don't shout.

THE INTERNET AND SIM CARDS

Internet is fast and reliable throughout most of the country, with 5G cellular services launched by two of the mobile network operators in 2020. Smartphones are ubiquitous, and Thailand is as ensconced in the digital age as anywhere else on Earth. Facebook is by far the most popular social media platform: the country has some 50 million registered users and is usually in the very top tier of users worldwide in terms of statistics. In addition to maintaining their individual profiles, Thais use Facebook to form groups, organize social events, buy and sell things, and represent their businesses, large or small. The free Thai messaging app Line is also universally popular. See page 194 for more apps that are worth downloading.

Thailand has three main mobile network operators: AIS, DTAC, and True Move. You can buy SIM cards all over the country very easily from a dealer or any 7-11, although as a foreigner you must register the SIM card with your passport. Many report that AIS has the best coverage.

The Thai postal service is surprisingly reliable, offering affordable registered delivery and tracking service.

MEDIA AND CENSORSHIP

The country has six terrestrial TV channels, most of which are owned by the army and the government, as well as countless satellite channels and radio stations. There is a very lively print media, especially relative to

the rest of Southeast Asia, with ten or so mass circulation daily newspapers of varying quality and a diversity of magazines about politics, culture, religion, sports, travel, etc. The two primary English language dailies are *The Bangkok Post* and *The Nation*.

Internet surveillance and media censorship has got steadily worse over the last few decades, primarily in regard to political commentary and activism. The print media still get away with frank and open commentary on almost everything except the monarchy.

CONCLUSION

A British diplomat, W.A.R. Wood, who came to Thailand as a young man in the last century, wrote a book entitled *Consul in Paradise*. Like countless before him, he fell in love with the country and its people and eventually came to settle in this "paradise."

After the rapid industrialization of recent years, however, there are fears that Thailand may soon become a paradise lost. Bangkok is no longer the tranquil city of canals that it was when Wood first arrived, and today one has to travel for hours from the capital to find quiet, secluded areas of natural beauty. Moreover, some fear that the color and singularity of Thai culture, in both its tangible and intangible forms, are becoming diluted, as the steamroller of globalization continues its seemingly relentless course.

Change is, of course, perfectly natural, and Thailand will continue to adapt to the pressures and problems of modernity as it has for centuries. Thai identity, with all the social and cultural diversity— and whose surface this book has only scratched—is resilient, and as historian Maurizio Peleggi points out, Thailand has always been a "worldly kingdom," its culture deeply shaped through interaction and engagement with the outside world. In many ways this is part of Thailand's charm. It is a rich and fascinating country, its people warm and welcoming, and for the time being at least, still possesses much of its natural splendor.

USEFUL APPS

Communication and Socializing

Eventbrite: See what events are on nearby when in Bangkok.

Line: Thailand's WhatsApp. If you want to message your Thai friends, you will need this app.

Longdo: Reliable English–Thai translation app. Type English or Thai.

Thai by Nemo: Free app for learning Thai. Includes audio for pronunciation.

Travel and Transport

Agoda/Booking: Either of these two hotel-booking apps are reliable and offer discounted rates in Thailand.

Air Visual: Get detailed air quality readings in most parts of the country. Useful in the dry season when the air quality in the north decreases dramatically.

Amazing Thailand: Official Tourist Authority of Thailand app with detailed info for every province.

Bangkok MRT: Journey planning app for Bangkok's subway system. Includes additional public transport information such as bus lines and moto-taxi stations.

BTS Skytrain: Bangkok's official Skytrain app includes info on routes, ticket prices, bus routes, and the city's major monuments.

Grab: Taxi app that affords peace of mind and convenience, and also delivers food. You can pay on delivery/arrival.

NOSTRA: Offline maps for all of Thailand. Includes route planning, points of interest, real time traffic information, and will inform you of all transport options for any chosen destination. English and Thai.

12goasia.com: Though a Web site not an app, well worth a mention. A one-stop shop to book boat, bus, train, and plane tickets for all over Asia.

Food and Shopping

Eatgio: Browse options and make reservations for restaurants in Bangkok, Pattaya, and Chiang Mai. Daily discounts available, and no credit card required for bookings.

Food Panda: Order food from nearby restaurants for delivery to your location. Pay on delivery option available.

Lazada: Southeast Asia's most popular online shopping platform.

FURTHER READING

Baker, Christopher and Pasuk Phongpaichit. *A History of Thailand*. Melbourne: Cambridge University Press, 2009.

Baker, Christopher and Pasuk Phongpaichit. *The Tale of Khun Chang Khun Paen: Siam's Great Folk Epic of Love and War*. Chiang Mai: Silkworm Press, 2012.

Cornwel-Smith, Philip and John Goss. *Very Thai: Everyday Popular Culture*. Bangkok: River Books, 2013.

Kitiarsa, Pattana. *Mediums, Monks and Amulets: Thai Popular Buddhism Today*. Chiang Mai: Silkworm Books, 2012.

Krairoek, Piraya. *Roots of Thai Art*. Bangkok: River Books 2012.

Lapcharoensap, Rattawut. *Sightseeing*. New York: Grove Atlantic, 2006.

Osborne, Lawrence. *Bangkok Days*. Vintage Books USA, 2010.

Osborne, Milton. *Southeast Asia. An Introductory History*. London: Allen & Unwin 2013.

Peleggi, Maurizio. *Thailand: The Worldly Kingdom*. London: Reaktion, 2007.

Smyth, David. *Teach Yourself Thai*. London: McGraw-Hill, 2003.

Thai Phrase Book and Dictionary. London: Berlitz, 2011

Wyatt, David K. *A Short History of Thailand*. Chiang Mai: Silkworm Press, 2004.

PICTURE CREDITS

INDEX

Acknowledgment

J. Rotheray wishes to acknowledge the work of the previous author of this book, Roger Jones, and also Parwinee Rotheray for her patient assistance.